Women as Educators

WOMEN AS EDUCATORS

Editors
Dr. Digumarti Bhaskara Rao
Ms. Digumarti Pushpa Latha
Ms. Digumarti Harshitha
Academy of Communication Culture
Education Science and Service
1-22-10 Srinivasa Nagar
Guntur—522006
Andhra Pradesh
India

DISCOVERY PUBLISHING HOUSE
New Delhi

Published by:
Tilak Wasan

DISCOVERY PUBLISHING HOUSE PVT. LTD.
4383/4B, Ansari Road, Darya Ganj
New Delhi-110 002 (India)
Phone : +91-11-23279245, 23253475, 43596065
E-mail : discoverypublishinghouse@gmail.com
sales@discoverypublishinggroup.com
web : www.discoverypublishinggroup.com

Edition: **2020**

ISBN: 978-81-7141-602-8

Women as Educators

Printed at:
Infinity Imaging Systems
Delhi

CONTENTS

WOMEN AS EDUCATORS

Cultural identity and family values are largely passed on to new generations by women. But, paradoxically, their access to education is limited in many parts of the world. Under this circumstance, UNESCO commissioned a study to make a comparative analysis of women as educators in the family, in the school, in the community and in the public life in the nine high-population countries known as E-9 (Bangladesh, Brazil, China, Egypt, India, Indonesia, Mexico, Nigeria and Pakistan) countries.

This study reveals that the progress in women's empowerment is perceptible in all the E-9 countries except Nigeria, though the commitment to women's empowerment is at best lukewarm. Many of these countries still believe that a woman's place is in the home and tend to restrict their activities to motherhood and household work. Evidence shows that presence of women teachers has a positive effect on enrolment. In rural areas of E-9 people still ignore the right to education for women and girls and in urban areas the family faces challenges from poverty and lack of access to basic social services. The educational level of parents, principally of mothers, is determining the educational achievement of their children. It is evident that the higher level of educational development of girls and women, the higher the indices of female empowerment. Women are felt essential in bringing the fundamental institutions—family, society and school—closer together to achieve a relevant and life-long education for all.

This study has been commissioned by Mr. Wolfgang Vollmann, E-9 Co-ordinator, UNESCO and this document, entitled Women as Educators and Women's Education in E-9 Countries, has been prepared by the Department for International Relations of the Mexican Ministry of Public Education based on the national studies of 'Women as Educators' provided by the members of the E-9 group of high-population countries and the National EFA 2000 Assessment Reports under the leadership of its Director-General Mrs. Sofialeticia Morales

Garga. The technical co-ordination was provided by Juan Christian Medina Campos and Ivett Navarro Ramirez, and the drafting and synthesis was done by Juan Christian Medina Campos, Ivett Navarro Ramirez, Tomas Nahul Munoz Barbosa and Angelica Tornero. Wolfgang Vollmann as editorial co-ordinator and Jean O'Sullivan, Hind Bidaoui and Mairead Maguire as editorial assistants supported this document from UNESCO Paris.

We are thankful to the authors, editors, the E-9 governments and UNESCO for reproducing the material in this book for the benefit of students, teachers, researchers educationists, policy makers and activists concerned to women education and empowerment.

Harshitha
Pushpa Latha
International Women's Day

PREFACE

Since 1993 the nine high-population countries (Bangladesh, Brazil, China, Egypt, India, Indonesia, Mexico, Nigeria and Pakistan) have committed themselves to promoting and achieving basic education for all. Special attention has been given to women as the majority of that group is still excluded from literacy and basic education. In this respect, this publication gives a most welcome account of women as educators in the E-9 countries.

It is an established fact that women constitute a major educating force in society, both in the traditional and modern senses of the word, but little credit is given to their contribution to the development of society. In 1995, the World Conference on Women, in Beijing, China, reasserted that no sustainable national development could ever be possible unless all women are given an equal right to education. In the light of ongoing national efforts, the E-9 countries launched a joint project on "women as educators" to identify those areas where women play a role and what it means in terms of educational efforts. The nine national studies commissioned by UNESCO cast a more comprehensive look at the role of women in society, especially at community level and in areas such as religion, neighbourhood life or NGO involvement. The studies reveal not only the considerable functional importance of women in society, but also the harsh facts of the exclusion of women from mainstream education.

The present synthesis study highlights the efforts made by the E-9 countries to make the education of women a top priority for national action. Reference is made to numerous local, provincial and national initiatives and programmes, which are being implemented, sometimes in the face of resistance. Major political parties, large NGOs and religious congregations, but also politicians and policy makers, have made the issue a permanent feature of their programmes. They have come to realise the immense potential of creativity and skills represented by women, and their irreplaceable and permanent role in society and national development.

The needs for modern development and the age-old educating role of women are cast against the exclusion of women from education. Data and graphs are used to illustrate the concrete facts of exclusion. The recent data based on the EFA 2000 assessment provided a very timely contribution to the analysis. This study has taken the most striking examples of nine national studies to question established patterns of thinking on women and education. From traditional, centuries-old structures to the needs of modern development where all members of society are entitled to education, the range is indeed large and authors have succeeded in covering the ground and establishing a bridge between societies of yesterday and of tomorrow.

W. Vollmann
E-9 Co-ordinator
UNESCO
Paris

INTRODUCTION

The undisputed role that education plays in the formation of a nation is clear. A good part of the cultural identity and national awareness of a people is passed on to new generations through, both formal and informal education. This is why governments invest so much in developing education programmes, training teachers, building more and better education centres. These governments are investing in their future, and the development of their people, in a world that is forever shrinking.

Ten years after The World Conference on Education for All in Jomitien (Thailand), in 1990 and seven years after the Delhi Summit of the E-9 countries (1993), the first results can be seen regarding literacy and the education of women and girls. In some regions, women's level of education has even surpassed that of men, while in others inequality is still widespread.

Women have gradually found their voice in their families, communities and even in public circles. They have thus become catalysts of social transformation, not more important than men, but rather with the same dignity and nature.

Yet there is still a great amount to be done to establish gender equality. The idea of women as educators, should permeate society. The educational efforts of governments should reach every village and town. In this way people will become more open and receptive to new ways of looking at the world and society.

The building of modern open societies, cannot only be the province of governments or international agencies, but rather has to be accompanied by society as a whole, thanks to the values transmitted by the family. The widely accepted importance of educating women is prerequisite for social transformation and national development.

This document describes the results of the efforts of the E-9 countries in this direction, which are very wide-ranging. Statistical data on education are included, as well as contextual indicators that may give a better idea of national policies to which the education figures belong (see educational and contextual indicators tables in Annex 1). The principal educational programmes developed in these countries are summarised in Annex 2.

Statistics tend to be a reflection of government intervention, and the tools by which governments can not only evaluate their actions, but also anticipate and attend to problems before they become unmanageable. In this respect, the E-9 governments have become fully aware of the need to have reliable statistics departments to maintain the viability of not only educational, but public programmes and plans in general.

What statistics frequently do not show is the diversity of populations, and consequently, the problems and solutions to providing education for all faced by each country. The E-9 countries have set an example to the world in the creation of innovative education programmes. Some new ways to attack old problems include educational caravans in the desert, that bring education to the most remote regions of Eygpt, housing schemes in China to attract trained teachers to the country's most far-flung rural areas, and the publication of textbooks and educational materials in indigenous languages.

No one can doubt the motivation of these governments, although there are still many shortfalls. Nobody questions the fact that the education of women is a catalyst in the educational development of these countries.

In order to make the comparative analysis of "women as educators" in the E-9 countries, a frame of reference was prepared for the preparation of national diagnoses. This benchmark included four objectives that were converted in fundamental lines of analysis:

1. **Women as educators in the family**
2. **Women as educators in school**
3. **Women as educators in the community**
4. **Women as educators in society**

It was not always possible for the countries to cover all of the indicators proposed in the base document, and therefore a final adjustment had to be made, by focusing on four different categories of indicators:

1. **Principal indicators, based on the National EFA 2000 Assessment Reports**
2. **Contextual educational indicators**
3. **Contextual socio-demographic indicators**
4. **Human development indicators**

Three more points should be made regarding the indicators.

1. It was not always possible to obtain precise information from all countries, which explains why some tables are incomplete.
2. In some documents, global rates were provided without data broken-down according to gender. However, with the additional qualitative and quantitative information, it was possible to complete the analysis and make a more detailed study.
3. Quantitative information was compared with the EFA 2000 Assessment Reports. It should be pointed out that when substantial differences existed, the data in the latest reports were used.

Countries were requested to provide data that illustrated gender inequality in rural areas, districts and municipalities, and in the most disadvantaged environments. Although no precise regional comparisons exist, diverse and valuable information regarding each country were submitted, including testimonies, examples and specific data, that clearly show that gender inequality is a reality, above all in the most marginalised or remote areas of the E-9 countries.

In the national studies on women, and the EFA 2000 Assessment, it is interesting to observe the following:

- In most countries compulsory schooling covers two levels of education and exceeds eight years.

Entrance age and duration of first and second level education

Country	Age																
	4	5	6	7	8	9	10	11	12	13	14	15	16	17	18	19	20
Bangladesh			1	2	3	4	5	6	7	8	9	10	11	12			
Brazil				1	2	3	4	5	6	7	8	9	10	11			
China				1	2	3	4	5	6	7	8	9	10				
Egypt			1	2	3	4	5	6	7	8	9	10	11	12			
India			1	2	3	4	5	6	7	8	9	10	11	12			
Indonesia				1	2	3	4	5	6	7	8	9	10	11	12		
Mexico			1	2	3	4	5	6	7	8	9	10	11	12			
Nigeria			1	2	3	4	5	6	7	8	9	10	11	12			
Pakistan		1	2	3	4	5	6	7	8	9	10	11	12				

First Level (primary). Second Level. Second Level, First Stage.
Second Level, Second Stage. 9 Compulsory Education

Source: Satistical Yearbook, UNESCO, 1998. National EFA-2000 Reports.

- Nigeria requires the fewest years of compulsory schooling (six years).
- In Indonesia, primary education starts at the earliest age (five).
- Brazil is the only case in which pre-university education consists of one single stage, with primary education having the longest duration (eight years).
- In Eygpt the duration of primary education was increased from 5 to 6 years in 1998. This means that total pre-university schooling is 12 years, plus 2 years of preschool.
- In Mexico compulsory education was increased from 6 to 9 years in 1993.

The nine countries analysed in this study share the challenge of addressing a large proportion of the world's illiterate population (70 per cent of the world total). Throughout the last decade, they have made unprecedented progress in making this population literate and instituting quality basic education for girls and women. Hand-in-hand with these advances has been a reduction of the population growth rates.

These countries, with identities forged over hundreds or thousands of years, have made a commitment to implement, promote and develop educational opportunities for all (men, women, girls and boys) while giving special consideration to women as the fundamental axis of development in any country.

"Educate a boy, educate a human being.

Educate a girl, educate several generations."

1

WOMEN AS EDUCATORS IN THE FAMILY

One of the principal roles of the family is to transmit values and attitudes to sons and daughters, with the aim of preserving the customs and habits of the group to which they belong and where they will often spend the rest of their lives.

Therefore, the family as a social institution ensures that children follow the behavioural guidelines and observe the ethical and moral standards that have guided previous generations.

However, this formerly clear situation has drastically altered throughout the 20th century as societies all over the world have become more complex. Causes include the rising degree of democratisation; which the recognition of difference and the right of individuals to defend their cultural diversity; demographic growth; the introduction of technology; to the awareness of individuality and economic and cultural globalisation.

In Mexico and Brazil, the family continues to be the fundamental nucleus of society; however, we can no longer talk about a single family model or homogenous way of life, as individuals have found ways to organise themselves which are different to conventional models[1].

The model in several Eastern and Middle Eastern countries is, of course, very different. Although the mother and father have traditionally formed an important nucleus, it has been a common practice to give members of the community, who are not blood relatives, certain responsibilities in the upbringing of children[2].

Even with the arrival of mass media: specifically television, radio and, at present, cybernetics—it is unquestionable that the family is the fundamental provider of education for children, together with formal education systems.

The arrival of communications technology—and the economic implications of its global reach—is favouring the globalisation of culture. Therefore, it is indispensable to teach people to read and write in their own language, to make them aware of their specificity so as to be able to value it and defend their culture.

Traditionally, women have been given the role of educators in the family, with the great responsibility of raising human beings with values and attitudes that help them in their individual and social lives. Paradoxically, their lack of information, training and access to education prevents them from making an optimum contribution to the development of self-assured, independent and self-sufficient individuals.

Mothers who possess little training and information in this complex world, educate their children without the tools required to face challenges in the fields of health, diet, social development and the preservation of identify.

This chapter makes a comparative analysis of the nine high population countries, or E-9 countries, related to the role of women as transmitters of attitudes in society and their major influence on girls' value systems, as well as the motivation they give them to attend and succeed in school and in life in general. Another aim of this chapter is to analyse the role of women as educators in passing on information to their daughters regarding marriage, pregnancy and fertility.

THE TRADITIONAL ROLE OF WOMEN IN THE FAMILY

Even with clear cultural and religious differences, the E-9 countries share many traditional ideas of women's role commonly associated with child rearing and staying at home. In Bangladesh, Pakistan, Nigeria, Egypt, India and Indonesia, gender inequality is much more marked[3] than it is in Mexico, Brazil and China, where women have already made important advances.

Although a legal framework exists that favours women in the education system, in the first group of countries, gender parity is difficult to achieve, due to beliefs that limits the level of empowerment that women can reach.

In Bangladesh, for example, people consider women's place is principally in the home, where their tasks are limited to bringing up children and carrying out domestic chores. Therefore, their success in life completely depends on the efficiency with which they play their role as wives and mothers[4].

People in Bangledesh consider that as women's knowledge is acquired through informal education, they do not need school, given that the education system does not offer the skills or knowledge suitable for carrying out the responsibilities of a mother. It is believed that the level of education of women should be lower than that of their husbands. It is also thought that educated daughter-in-laws are less willing to adopt the rules, values and discipline of the in-laws[5]. This inferior status of women is related to the traditional role they play in the family and in society.

Reasons for sending sons and daughters to school are based on the same value system. The idea that women should better themselves in other fields than the home is not very widespread. For a change to take place, parents must raise their expectations for their daughters, who in turn must be made more aware of their potential by developing their skills.

In Bangladesh, Nigeria, Indonesia, Pakistan, India and Egypt, the obstacles to sending sons and daughters to school transcend mere physical obstacles or the need to keep girls at home fetching water and doing other basic tasks. In these countries the problems are more complex. Ideological, religious and cultural factors legitimise the arrangements found by families or societies to meet their basic needs, although these arrangements cause the marginalisation of women. This situation makes it difficult to implement programmes that promote equal opportunities. Religious education is extremely influential and the values that are handed down from generation to generation are not questioned.

Several national evaluation documents indicate that some of the established customs that limit the possibilities of women's empowerment differ from those of Islam.

In Egypt, there is a strong recognition of the crucial role of women in sustainable development, and the Eqyptian government is publicly committed to integrating them into this process. However, inequality is evident in some social and political environments, and has diverse impacts on the life of women from different social classes, limiting their access to education and jobs, as well as their inclusion in the decision-making process.

Most Egyptian women stay at home and only go out for work if the need is pressing. They have to abide by strict moral standards as an example for the other members of the family. They are also characterised by their spirit of self-sacrifice in the family.

In Pakistan, women play an important role in the education of the family, inspired fundamentally by Islam. The most important contribution of women is in the teaching of the Koran, which they see as the ultimate Divine Book and code of conduct. Currently, it is estimated that around 60 per cent of Pakistani women are literate in the Koran. Most of these women, in both urban and rural areas, teach the Koran to their children or work in mosques or other temples. In rural areas, above all, women grand-mothers, mothers and aunts, are fundamental cultural educators; they are the source of information, education and training in topics such as fertility, pregnancy, nutrition, hygiene and health.

In ancient times, India had women educators who were brilliant academics and disciples. However, subsequent traditions related to the dharma or code of ethics, along with successive uprisings and invasions, led to the decline of the social role of women. The age of consent for women fell and no institutional platform for their education was built[6].

Although during the colonial years several efforts were made to build an educational structure for women, the reality is that no work was carried out until independence.

In Indonesia, the 1945 Constitution enshrines the principle of equality between men and women; however, women and girls still face great obstacles in access to education. Although women work on different projects, they are not considered as indispensable. For example, in concrete production projects promoted by the government in marginalised areas, only men are considered as full participants even though women they spend the same time and effort[7]. For women to advance in the educational field in Indonesia, there must be a change made in attitudes towards them at the level of decision-making, planning and leadership.

Nigerian women are responsible for feeding, dressing and caring for both girls and boys, for their socialisation and integration into the community, and for instructing them in their own cultural standards. In traditional Nigerian communities, the school is society as a whole, where the educators are parents, members of the extended family and the community. The father also plays in important role in the moral guidance of his children: he is in charge of teaching them customs and traditions. Grandmothers, aunts and other women are responsible for the mother and the newborn baby during the first days of life. In some polygamous homes the first wife supervises the other wives and children. This is especially notable in the Hausa culture, in which the children born of other women are taken to the first wife, who educates them. In Nigeria, the value of religions such as Christianity and Islam is not ignored. The coexistence of formal education and religious education is considered important.

China, Brazil and Mexico differ from the other countries in urban areas; however, in rural, marginalised and remote communities, women's role is, in several similar to the other countries.

For thousands of years, China was a country in which patriarchal society prevailed, and where the values based on confucianism had a great influence on the perception of women, both by men and by women themselves. The idea that men are above women because the sky is above the earth has prevailed for years. Traditionally, according to the "Three Obediences" doctrine, when a woman is young she depends on her father and brothers; when she marries, she depends on her husband, and when her husband dies, she depends on her sons. The role of woman used to be limited to child-rearing. As in all the E-9 countries, the mother is very important in the education of her sons and daughters, but in China this role not only arises from the natural relationship, it is also covered by Confucian philosophy.[8]

China—unlike other Asian countries—has given importance in recent years to the education and empowerment of women. Traditionally, the maternal influence over sons and daughters has justified the education of women. Perhaps this tradition is the reason why, in this country, the educational advances of women and girls have been so evident.

In the last few years, Brazil has seen a great change in the values of the rigid patriarchal hierarchies of yesteryear, both in relationships between the sexes and between generations. Women also have more options to work and have an influence in public life. Furthermore, men are encouraged to have more responsibility in educating their children. However, these values have changed principally among the middle classes, with higher levels of education among people in urban areas and in the South Eastern and Southern regions[9].

The number of homes in which the mother is the head of the family is high and, in many cases, these families are poor. Women who live on the outskirts of cities, obliged to work in order to support the family, have found alternative childcare by creating community circles. These women are the sole educators of their children, as the father is absent.

In Mexico dramatic changes can be seen in women's role in society due, among other causes, to demographic changes, the increase in girls at school and the incorporation of women into the job market. However, the traditional roles of women in the family persist, above all in rural areas, where stereotypes limit the work of women to the field of reproduction and the home in order to bring up and educate their children. Until fifty or sixty years ago, even in the urban environment, women were only prepared for marriage, irrespective of their level of schooling. The idea that women are only good for having children still permeates the mentality of Mexican men who have a low level of education—the more children they have, more proof they have of their own manhood.

In the rural environment, this idea of women's role still prevails. Parents see daughters in school as an expense, and not as an investment. In the poorest rural communities, with few services, girls have to help in the home, which distracts them from their education; their first duty consists of helping their mothers with domestic chores. However, there has been an outstanding increase in female schooling in marginalised rural areas in a very short time.

Mexico, Brazil and China have certain similarities. The ground that women have gained in relation to men, above all in urban areas, is not able. Although a lot of work still needs to be done, it is clear that significant advances have been made. More and more women—and men—consider that their daughters, along with their sons, should receive a proper formal education.

The fact that Brazil and Mexico secularised public life many years ago has allowed the separation of religious and governmental institutions. This has strengthened the idea of citizenship as a shared state, with the same responsibilities and rights enjoyed by all individuals. Notwithstanding these advances, there are still social sectors and geographical areas in these countries where women are unable to put them into practice.

WOMEN IN THE SHAPING OF VALUE SYSTEMS

In E-9 countries, women play a fundamental role in the shaping of values, in many different ways.

In Egypt, women are a vital influence in the first five years of their children's lives. The methods of bringing up and educating children differ clearly between educated mothers and illiterate ones. Many studies prove that educated mothers are more able to adapt to social and economic changes, they are aware of their rights and duties, they benefit from health, cultural and social services and are thus able to improve the life of their families and children. They are also keen to teach them moral values[10]

It is important to point out that Islam does not segregate women, and claims that work and study are compulsory for both sexes. In ancient Egypt, as in ancient times in India, women actively participated in economic and social life[11].

In Pakistan, women are considered as the principal transmitters of values and therefore their conduct, following their cultural and religious guidelines, must be irreproachable.

In Bangladesh, women provide education on values and norms, on religious matters, health practices and domestic work, principally in rural areas[12]. Mothers influence the conduct of their sons and daughters during early childhood, but have more influence over the girls, who stay at home while the sons tend to go with their fathers. The Bangladesh evaluation document indicates that boys show greater independence, and their behaviour is curious and exploratory. Girls are repressed if they speak out loud, while in boys this is considered a virtue. Parents value malleability and a co-operative attitude in their daughters but disapprove of assertiveness. In boys, they seek independence, assertiveness and a questioning attitude; fear and shyness in boys are unacceptable. Consequently, children adopt values before entering school. This phenomenon is shared, to differing degrees, by the majority of E-9 countries. A study in Bangladesh[13] found that mothers play a central role in shaping values and attitudes in both daughters and sons, and that the father principally played the role of "administrator."

In India, women have an important role as educators in the family. The education they give their daughters establishes the values of service and obedience. The same occurs in Indonesia, where women are considered as having less rights than men. The values that these women, most of them illiterate, pass on to their daughters, make it difficult for these girls to achieve empowerment.

In Nigeria, women teach and pass on values, but the responsibility is shared. As we have seen, in some rural areas the first wife takes charge of the children of the husband's other wives, and is supported by the extended family and by the community. In fact, upon adolescence, they cease to be the responsibility of the family and become the responsibility of the community. Nigerian mothers have the task of initiating their sons and daughters in the tasks of the home. These tasks may be sweeping the house, washing the plates, lighting the fire, carrying water or firewood, looking after small brothers and sisters, looking after animals, cooking, etc. The father provides both girls and boys with discipline, and is responsible for supervising their moral and vocational education.

In China, educational advances have been truly remarkable. However, differences exist between Eastern and Western China, between rural and urban areas, between poor and rich areas, and between the different entities. Illiteracy is highest in the western part of China, where a dozen minorities inhabit cold and remote places, in mountainous areas with poor conditions and low productivity rates.

In traditional Maxican society, mainly in rural indigenous areas, mothers still pass on values to their daughters on behaviour and attitudes. The values of submission and obedience, of unconditional support and dependence on men are handed down from generation to generation. Part of the identity of Maxican women is influenced by the idea that femininity has no place in the public environment and that women's fulfilment must be confined to the privacy of their own homes. Here, fathers transmit values to sons and mothers to daughters, although, paradoxically, the preferential treatment given by mothers to the men becomes a weapon used against their daughters, who will later be wives.

Although gender parity improved significantly in Mexican society in the second half of the 20th century, the notion of male superiority is passed on by women themselves to their sons and daughters, if not overtly, then through their attitudes.

The upbringing girls receive in the family has important consequences: notably exclusion from social and public life and a low level of empowerment. As in Brazil, in Mexico different forms of family organisation coexist. Currently, many women are heads of families and are responsible for supporting their children; on occasions they ask other families to look after their sons or daughters. Diverse links are thus organised, as well as different perceptions of the tasks of the mother.

In Brazil, women are important in shaping values in girls and boys; however in urban, marginalised areas there has been an increase in homes in which women are the heads of the family. These women, who are totally responsible for their sons and daughters, must also seek a way of supporting the family, and therefore are forced to leave them in the care of other persons or State institutions. This has caused changes in values and in how they are passed on.

In Brazil, in rural areas, the education and socialisation of girls and boys belongs to women, who appear in surveys as the central figures of the family[15]. However, the work carried out on farms or in the home is not valued either socially or economically. These women, like those in rural areas in E-9 countries, have very low levels of schooling.

The media, in both Brazil and in Mexico, play a very important role in the passing on of values, principally in urban sectors, and get a mixed reaction from the population[14].

Both countries have been greatly influenced by technology and communications, which has meant that life in general has become more complex. The phenomenon of globalisation has brought with it great advantages, but also serious problems. One of them is the broadcasting of different values. The mother and father may need to receive the support of the school, the media and other institutions, in order to preserve universal values in societies that are undergoing constant change.

In these countries, the transmission of values is made more complex because they are heterogeneous: the traditional rural family, even the indigenous family, in the case of Mexico, is not the same as the urban poor family. In the latter, for example, girls and boys, forced to work, move from childhood to adulthood in a family environment that is not always suitable for their development.

WOMEN'S LITERACY AND GIRLS' EDUCATION

Preschool

Education should be considered as a living process and not as a voluntary choice by authorities and parents. Great responsibility is attached to deciding whether girls and boys should enter school, and that responsibility should be shared by both men and women. However, in order for education to really fulfil its objectives, it is necessary to eliminate the school-home dichotomy. The teaching given in education centres should not be reduced to a parcel of knowledge that over time end up being useless, but should help to develop and promote skills and abilities that are useful throughout life. Preference should be given to quality over quantity.

Although part of the need to provide preschool education to girls and boys under six years of age is due to economic, social and labour-related causes, the main reason consists of the importance of giving small children the skills that will allow them to fully benefit from their subsequent education.

Preschool is not attractive to the most traditional societies in some E-9 countries, who consider that children under five years old should be looked after by their mothers; in others, it is appreciated although, it has yet to operate on a global basis.

In China, early childhood education is considered very important in preparing more efficient students; however, the support it receives is minimal. For example, according to a survey carried out in 1996 in Zhen Feng, in the province of Guizhou, almost 100 per cent of the 4,778 students that repeated grades and over 95 per cent of the 875 who dropped out before 3rd grade, never received preschool education. Among the over 13000 students who passed the same grades, less

Graph 1: Gross rate of preschool enrolment[16] at the end of the nineties

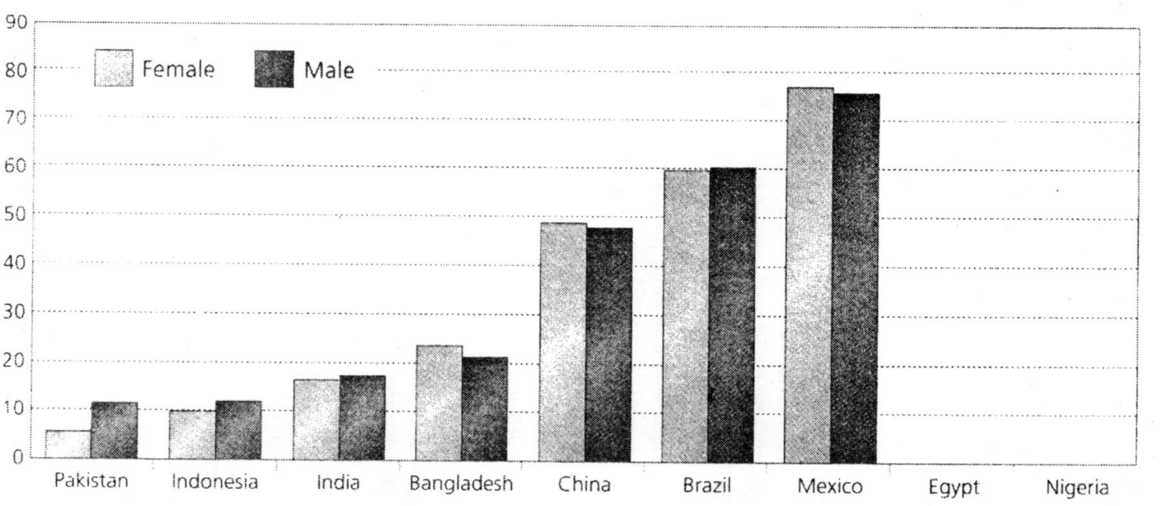

Source: National Reports on the EFA-2000 Assessment.

than one per cent had not had access to preschool education. However, the total coverage of 3-to-5 year olds was less than 50 per cent.

In China there are 181,368 preschool education centres, with an approximate enrolment of 24 million. The gross enrolment rate of children from 3 to 6 years of age rose from 39.7 per cent in 1996, to 42.7 per cent in 1997, with a gross girls rate of 48.6 per cent and a boys rate of 47.7 per cent. However, in an analysis of the rural areas in China, it can be observed that the percentage of enrolment in preschool education is very low, due to at least two reasons: people consider it unnecessary to send their children to school before the age of six and there are not enough official schools in any case.

In Egypt, preschool education gets support from the government and parents. Most preschool centres are in urban areas; the percentage in rural areas in very low. Childcare centres from 0-3 years are affiliated to the Ministry of Social Affairs, and different NGOs and private sectors. Kindergardens accept children from 3 to 6 years, but enrolment in the official preschool centres is low. Recently a decree was issued declaring two years of kindergarden as part of basic education. In Egypt, 10 per cent of boys and girls attend official preschool centres, which speaks about the need of development of this level of education.

Mexico and Brazil, countries with lower rural population rates, have greater preschool education coverage. In Mexico the rates are higher than in Brazil, which has a smaller rural population (Mexico, 26.5 per cent Brazil, 20 per cent). This may be a reflection of the relevance of the preschool education programmes implemented in these areas.

Preschool education in Brazil was incorporated into the education system by the 1988 Constitution. By 1998, 59.6 per cent of girls and 60.2 per cent of boys under five attended preschool. The rate is still low; there are very few official childcare centres, and not all mothers afford to their children to private ones. Women in poor urban areas, who need to work, have created family and community childcare networks, not always with the desired quality of education and care. Religious and community centres also exist, as well as philanthropic childcare organisations; however, such organisations do not have sufficient funds, and consequently provide their services under precarious conditions.

In Mexico, Article 37 of the General Education Act establishes

Graph 2: New enrolment 1st primary grade with preschool late nineties

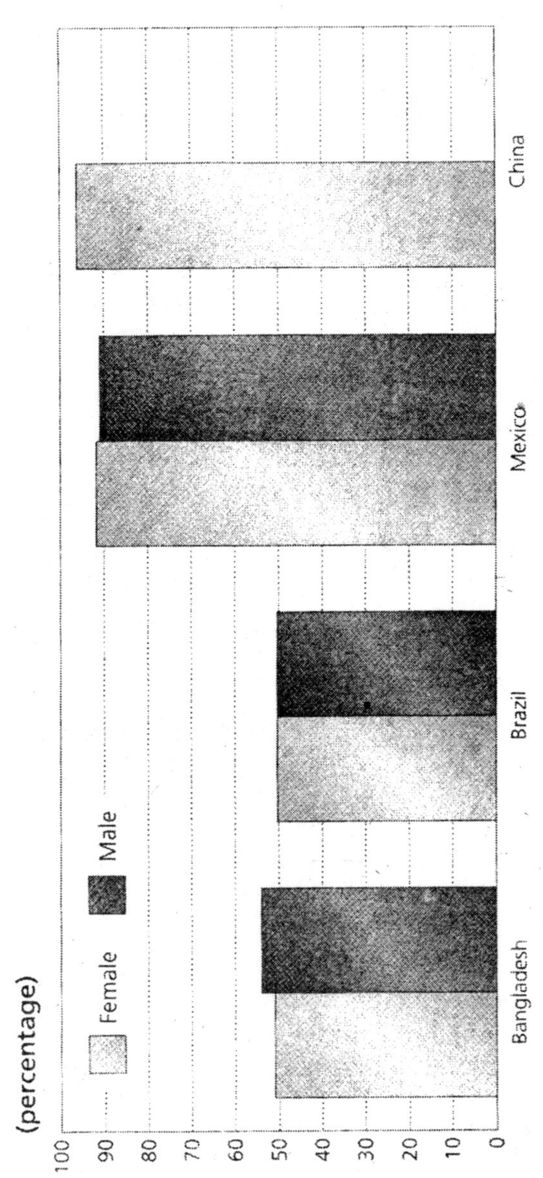

Source: National Reports on the EFA-2000 Assessment.

that early childhood education, along with primary and secondary schooling, form part of basic education[17]. This level caters for children between 3 and 5 years old and generally covers three grades. It is not compulsory and enrolment in the second or third year is possible. It is not a requirement to enter primary school. However, it should be noted that for the Mexican state at least one year of preschool education is obligatory; therefore almost 77 per cent of all girls and boys between the ages of 3 and 5, go to preschool.

In the other E-9 countries, this level of education is yet to be developed. In Nigeria, by 1990 only 4.7 per cent of preschool age boys and girls had access to this level of education. It is estimated today that this will have risen to 24.71 per cent. It is still believed that girls and boys under six should remain with their families. However, it should pointed out that the need for childcare centres exists, due, among other causes, to the increase in urbanisation and the fact that more and more women seek paid work. Currently, childcare centres in Nigeria are run by the private sector[18].

In Bangladesh, China and Mexico, the rate of this level of schooling is higher for girls than for boys, but in Pakistan the girls' rate is half the boys' rate.

Graph 2 shows the rates of several countries, related to boys and girls entering primary school after preschool education.

The graph[19] shows that for Bangladesh entry to primary school is less common for girls. In the case of Mexico it can be seen that the rate is slightly higher for girls. China not only shows a high primary school entry rate, it also has the highest net primary school enrolment rate (98.9 per cent) for girls. Mexico is second in the net girl enrolment rate. These two examples indicate that the greater the access to preschool, the greater the probability of access and survival in primary school.

All the education systems analysed here reflect the fact that the family and preschool school co-operate in order to guarantee the best early education of girls and boys under six years of age.

Primary Education

Primary education in E-9 countries has developed at great speed: in many countries net primary school enrolment rates are close to a hundred per cent. Legislation has established the free and compulsory nature of basic education. However, school survival rates and the achievement of basic literacy and numeracy skills are not always a reality. In many cases, girls are disadvantaged[37].

In the decade 1990-2000 the access of girls to primary education increased, thanks to a wide range of policies that include the adaptation of the national curriculum to the specific characteristics of marginalised or minority population groups; the application of programmes to provide additional funding to the poorest families; education systems and partnerships between society (the community, families and women) to guarantee the right of all to education.

These measures, often preceded by legal reforms, reflect the will of governments not only to increase the scope of education systems, but also to increase the quality, relevance and efficiency of the service.

In rural areas, cities and in all socio-economic classes, the existence of a partnership between the school and the family is fundamental for the development of children's intelligence. The ambitions that mothers have for the children usually determine their degree and form this-takes, more so than those of the father.

A mother with a high level of schooling will have greater knowledge of challenges, dangers and opportunities in the social and natural environment, which gives her the possibility to formulate effective and efficient strategies in promoting the development of her sons and daughters. The higher the level of education of mothers and fathers, the higher the expectations they have for their sons and daughters, and the clearer their objectives.

In China, 80 per cent of the mothers and fathers questioned in the provinces of Gansu, Ningxia, Qinghai and Guizhou agreed that their daughters should attend school, but when asked to what grade they would like them to study, their levels of schooling became evident[20]. A table presenting the results of this investigation is revealing. To the question "to what grade should your sons and daughters go to school?", the option "Not considered" was given by 32 per cent of illiterate mothers and fathers; 18.2 per cent of mothers and fathers;18.2 per cent of mothers and fathers with level 1 of primary school; 16 per cent of mothers and fathers with level 2; 8.2 per cent of mothers and fathers with grade 1 of secondary school; and 2.8 per cent of mothers and

Graph 3: Female literacy and girls education[26] at the end of the nineties

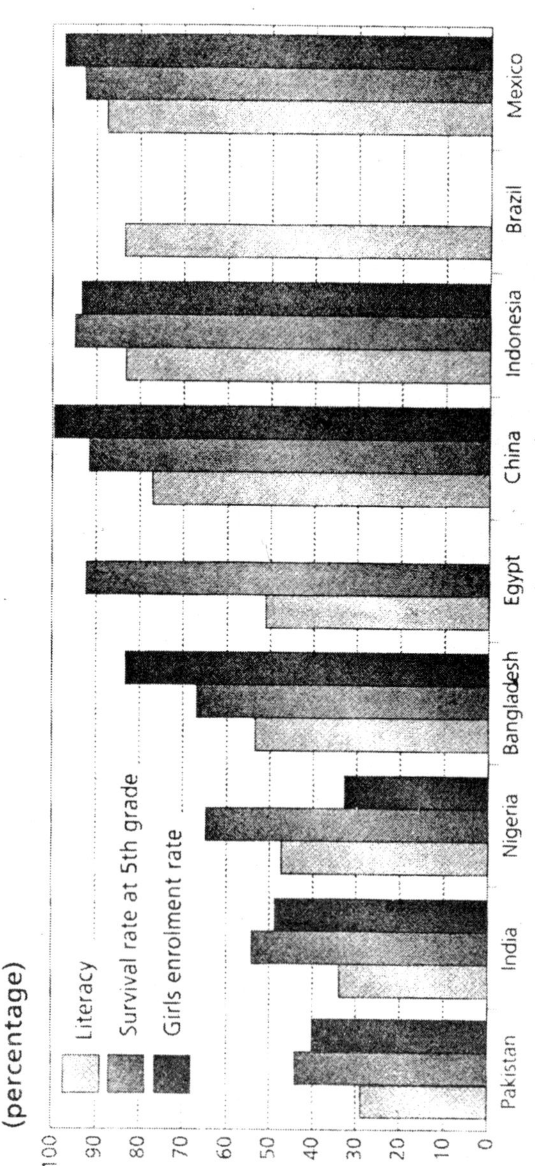

Source: National Reports on the EFA-2000 Assessment.

fathers with grade 2 level of secondary school. This indicates that the lower the grade of schooling of parents, the less developed an idea they have of why they send their children to school and the lower their expectations of their children. On the other hand, mothers and fathers with secondary school level studies have high expectations for their sons and daughters.

In a poll carried out in 1992 and 1993 on 2,644 illiterate women in ten Chinese provinces, it was found that 57.9 per cent of their fathers and 86.2 per cent of their mothers were illiterate or semi-illiterate. In families where both parents are illiterate, it is practically impossible for the children to receive proper education.

In Egypt, illiterate mothers and fathers equip their children less for life. Illiteracy has an impact on their creed, attitude, behaviour and the decisions they make. The mother's education has a definite impact in terms of increasing the probability that girls will go to school and finish primary education[21].

Illiterate parents may decide in favour of an early marriage for their daughters, forcing them to drop out of school. While in Cairo the female literacy rate reaches 76.9 per cent, in the rural areas of Egypt it is 28.3 per cent[22]. In this country female illiteracy (48.9 per cent) is almost double the rate of male illiteracy (26 per cent). In 1993 there were 600,000 girls aged between 6 and 10 out of school, above all in rural and poor areas.

A study carried out in Bangladesh shows that 57.5 per cent of sons and daughters of families in which both parents have studied up to secondary education or higher, attend school. In homes where they have only attended primary school, 17.5 per cent attend school, while in homes where the father is illiterate, only 5 per cent attend[23]. In this same study it was found that 95 per cent of women educate their children regarding health and hygiene, while only 60 per cent of men do so. All the mothers give greater importance to religious and ethical matters in the development of this children, while 70 per cent of men take care of this aspect.

A study on enrolment and retention in primary education indicates that many parents are unaware of the importance of their sons and daughters attending school. It is considered to be more expensive to send girls to school given that they have to be replaced

Graph 4: Literacy

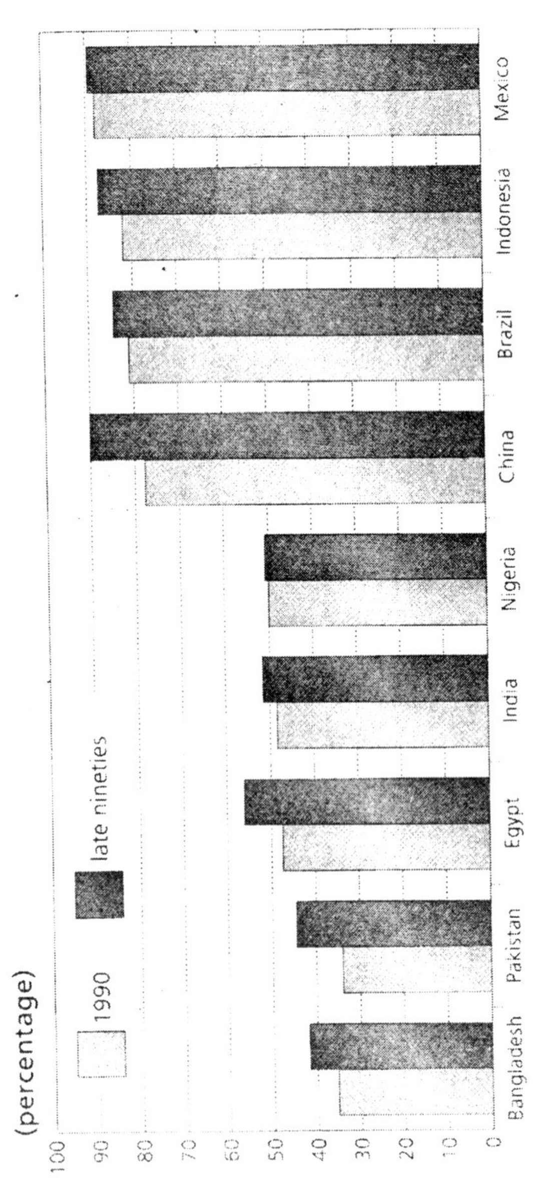

Source: National Reports on the EFA-2000 Assessment.

Graph 5: Female literacy and female net enrolment rate in primary education at the end of the nineties

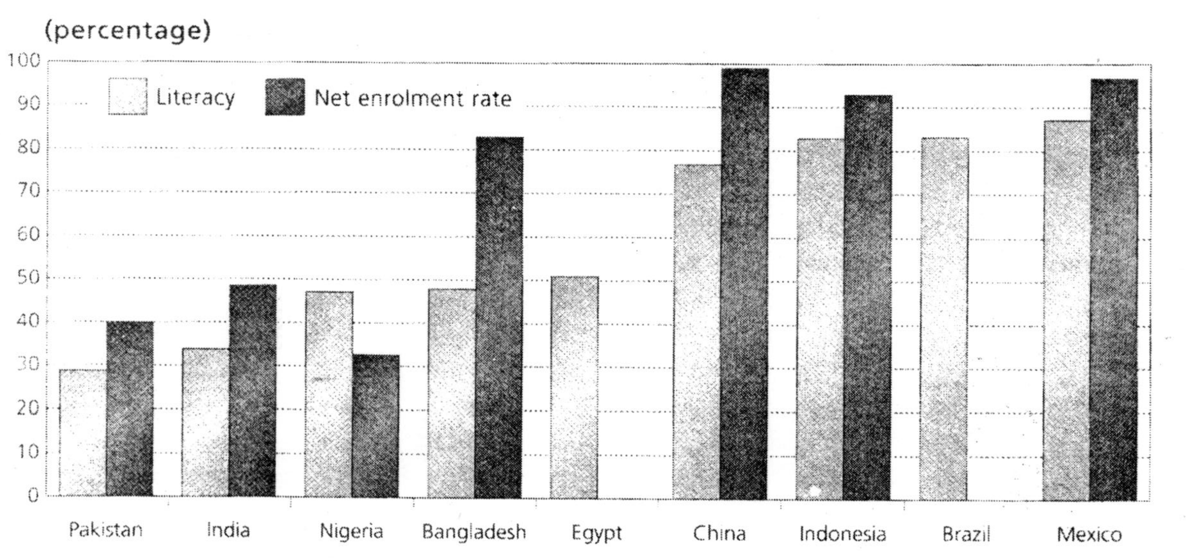

Source: National Reports on the EFA-2000 Assessment.

by domestic help, who must be paid[24]. Another element that contributes to girls dropping out of school is the average age of marriage, which is 17.

In 1998 a poll was made of the most outstanding students in secondary schools in Bangladesh. All of them indicated that one of the most important reasons for their school success was the encouragement they received from their parents, especially their mothers[25].

In E-9 countries, the relationship between the role of mothers and the educational success of their children, especially girls, can be seen when looking at female literacy and the female 5th grade survival rate, shown in the above graph.

The higher the level or reading and writing in a society and, principally, the use of written language by the mother, the greater the stimulus at home that favours the educational success of children.

The case of Egypt is relevant, given that despite having a low female literacy rate, the survival rate of girls in school is very high.

Countries with the lowest 5th grade survival rates such as Pakistan, India and Nigeria, are also the ones with the lowest female literacy rates and the lowest schooling roles.

It is important to underline the fact that in most countries girls have lower drop-out rates than boys, which means that more of them reach 5th grade.

China presents the highest net girls' enrolment rates and a higher 5th grade survival rate for girls than for boys. In Brazil girls remain longer in school and sit more exams to pass to the next grade. Both sexes have serious dropout and repetition problems; however, girls perform better; fewer girls abandon school and fail exams[27]. From the age of seven, the proportion of students who are not in the grade corresponding to their age is higher for boys (14.7 per cent) than for girls (13 per cent)[28].

In Indonesia, the survival rate for girls is 94.3 per cent, while for boys it is 93.5 per cent. In Mexico the completion rate of girls is higher than that of boys in primary, secondary and high school. In the 1997-1998 school year, the failure rate of boys in primary school was 8.4 per cent and 6.1 per cent for girls; the boys' dropout rate for boys on this level was 3 per cent and that of girls 2.7 per cent[29]. The last national census in Mexico, in 1997, demonstrated that in the 15-to-18 year-old age range, the educational development of women is already superior to that of men.

The different levels of literacy among the adult population can be observed in graph 4, reflecting the development of basic education in each country, especially prior to the 1990s. The levels of literacy illustrate the difficulties faced by national education systems in reaching the unreached: linguistic minorities, traditional agricultural societies, remote and isolated communities. The above can be seen in graph 5, in the correlation between levels of female literacy and those of net girls' enrolment rates in primary education.

The fact that enrolment rates exceed literacy rates in nearly all countries does not contradict the hypothesis that the educational level of the mother has a determining influence on the education of her sons and daughters, but rather illustrates the government's effort to take basic education to new generations in places where previously no services existed. It is precisely this effort that explains why the advance of basic education in the new generations is higher than adult literacy. In China and Bangladesh the distance between both indicators shows the considerable effort made to extend the coverage of basic education. In Bangladesh, in 1993, a programme was initiated called Universal Primary Education that had among its goals, basic education for the 15.4 million girls and boys between the ages of 6 and 10. The great advances made in schooling in this country should be evaluated taking into consideration the fact that primary schooling was only made compulsory in 1992.

In Mexico, on the other hand, although the increases in school enrolment have not been extraordinary, they have implied a great efforts in terms of adapting curricula and compensatory financing, actions necessary for population groups who could benefit from traditional forms of basic education (rural ethnic-language groups, disabled children and remote communities which represent approximately 10 per cent of the population.)

In the last few years, regression in basic education in Nigeria is reflected in the fact that the net enrolment rate of girls in primary schools is lower than the female literacy rate. This fact is extraordinary in the context of the nine countries in question. If this trend is not reversed, the educational levels of the new generations will be lower than that of previous generations. In 1995, 25.09 per cent of girls who should have enroled in school, did not. Great inequality also exists in the development of secondary levels of education.

Nigeria has a high school dropout rate. For example, in 1995 it was reported that the average primary school completion rates for boys and girls were 56.3 per cent and 43.7 per cent, respectively. Most girls leave school due to inability to pay costs, distance or inaccessibility, religious factors, early marriage or sickness[30].

Any analysis of the advances of shortfalls stated in the national indicators should be accompanied by a reading of the disparities within societies, which gives us a clearer vision of the challenges faced in each country.

In China145 million people aged 15 and above are illiterate: 90 per cent of them live in rural areas and 70 per cent are women. In rural areas, rigid gender roles prevent women from access to education and their full insertion. Furthermore, most of the rural population in this country belongs to 49 ethnic groups who live in the west and have the lowest education rate[31]. In several Chinese provinces, principally in rural areas, the school dropout rate of girls is high (20.5 per cent) due to difficulty in reaching the school, as well as religious and traditional aspects. However, the general dropout rate in primary school is relatively low (0.93 per cent), with inequalities only appearing in the regional studies. In 1998, general primary school enrolment was 98.9 per cent, but only 19 provinces exceeded this indicator, while 12 were below it. Nearly 1.4 million school-age children did not attend school in 1997 and of them 1.03 million live in the 12 disadvantaged provinces. In certain regions, such as Tibet, the general dropout rate in primary education reaches 5.02 per cent, and that of girls, 6.80 per cent[32].

One of the reasons for low girls' attendance in primary school is the fact that in provinces such as Ningxia there are few female teachers and fewer still female principals. Studies have proven that the more female principals there are, the more female teachers and female students. For example, in Hui in 3,330 primary schools there are only 395 female teachers. Due to this, enrolment in primary education in this area is under 40 per cent. In mountainous areas, schools are far from homes, so that higher level students must go and live at the

Graph 6: Female literacy and rural population[42] at the end of the nineties

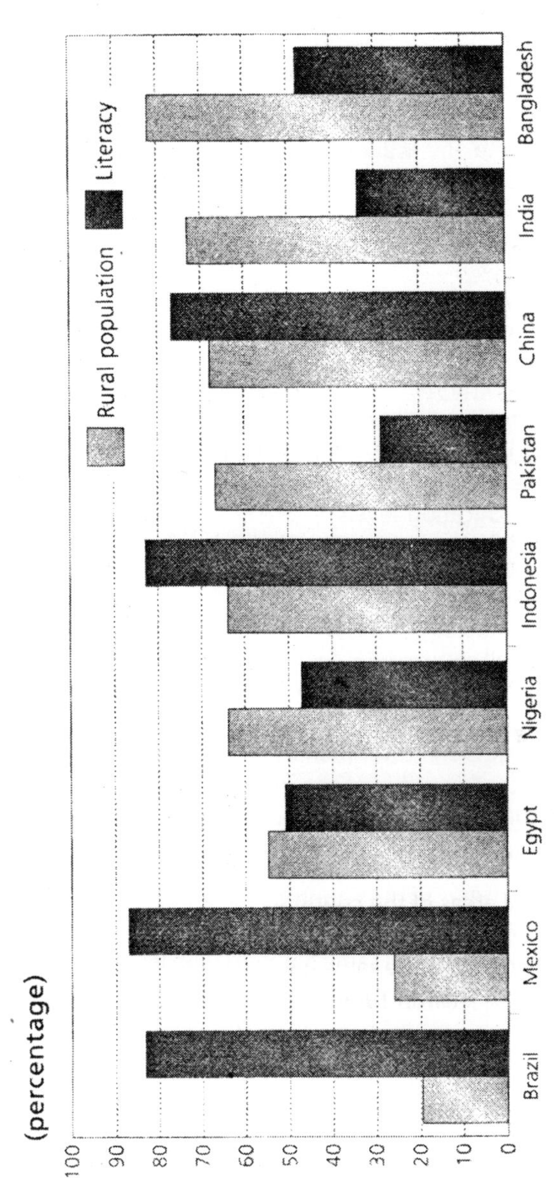

Source: National Reports on the EFA-2000 Assessment.

school; mothers and fathers are generally against their daughters leaving home.

In Mexico the rural and dispersed nature of the population is associated with educational marginalisation.The challenges are greater when these variables appear in communities belonging to one of the indigenous groups that speak one of the 80 languages and different dialects[33]. Generally, the regions where the indigenous communities are concentrated are found in the South East of the country, in the states of Oaxaca, Guerrero and Chiapas. In many indigenous communities, fifty per cent of women do not master reading and writing in Spanish.

In Brazil, girls who live in urban areas do not face problems entering school. However, in the North and among North East of Brazil, in the rural areas and the Afro-Brazilian population, illiteracy rate are much higher. The fact should be emphasised that, contrary to trends in other countries, female literacy in higher than male literacy (see graph 19). Since the eighties it is common to find more women than men in higher education levels[34].

In India, until 1951, the female literacy rate was only 7.93 per cent and Unesco estimated that by 1995 it would be 37.7 per cent. Notwithstanding, government efforts, the gap between female and male literacy is still very wide, as for men the rate is 70.5 per cent while for women it is 43.9 per cent. In the three most vulnerable states of India, U.P., Bihar and Rajasthan, with a population of 300 million in total, female literacy rates are lower than the national level. There are more than 100 districts (one fifth of the country) where levels of female literacy are under 10 per cent[35]. At the other extreme is Kerala where literacy levels are on a par with developed countries.

In the rural areas of the country, such inequality is very marked. While in urban areas 90.9 per cent of girls enrol in school, in rural areas only 69.8 per cent do so. The same happens with female literacy, which is higher in urban than in rural areas.

In Bangladesh, the national school dropout rate is very high among boys (14.8 per cent) and girls (17.2 per cent). However, this rate does not show the full panorama, given that in the rural environment these figures are double[36]. Dropout among girls is related to their social status, as well as the lack of access to remote schools and the demand for help in domestic tasks.

In general, the Northern states of Nigeria have lower enrolment rates than those in the South. For example, in 1995, while in Delta 52.43 per cent of girls were in primary school, in the North, in Sokoto, there were only 23.99 per cent.

In addition to national efforts to finance and reform education systems, in the last few years many E-9 countries have obtained financing from international organisations in order to build more schools and train more teachers.

Basic education has been accompanied by new adult education strategies. Both actions constitute a policy of universalisation of basic education. The efforts to provide relevant and good quality education to mothers and fathers are based on the assumption that boys and girls will receive encouragement at home for their own educational success; and the extension of basic education to early childhood will make it easier for literacy actions to penetrate.

In graph 6 the inverse relationship between the rural population and female literacy can be seen. Indonesia and China, countries with high rural populations and relatively high female literacy rates and net girls schooling rates, are exceptions to the rule. This correlation will be examined in further depth in the next paragraphs, including the reading of other variables.

SATISFYING BASIC NEEDS AND THE SUCCESS OF GIRLS IN SCHOOL

In precarious conditions, all the members of a family have to work to survive. Children take part in domestic and productive activities that allow that family to obtain basic goods and services. Unfortunately, in the poorest communities of the E-9 countries, the need for child labour is so great that boys and girls can neither access, remain or succeed in school. The involvement of children in the productive effort of families sometimes favours the formation of values and the acquisition of basic skills. However, in marginalised urban areas, for example, poverty and the absence of a family on force children to abandon school and join the growing group of homeless children. In the most marginalised and remote rural areas of the E-9 countries, the lack of basic services in the community, such as drinking water, fuel and food, force the family to employ girls and boys in collection and transport activities. When the family can be self-sufficient, the

Graph 7: Female literacy, female life expectancy, rural population and female population as percentage of total[41] at the end of the nineties

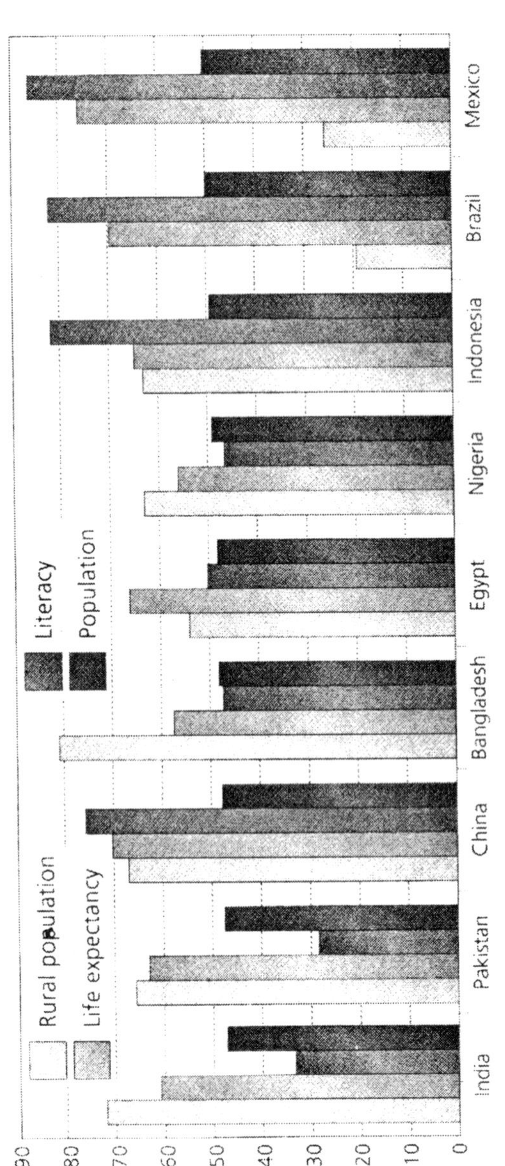

Source: National Reports on the EFA-2000 Assessment.

participation of children is considered indispensable. In extreme cases where they do not possess or have access to a plot of land, the family group usually sells its labour to agro-industrial corporations, which frequently requires temporary or definitive migration to the regions where this demand exists. In these cases, the regular attendance of girls and boys to school is impossible. Generally faced with these difficult situations, the rural family gives priority to the access of boys to school[38].

In the most remote areas of Pakistan, where it is difficult to get access for goods and services, most of the time and energy of women and girls is used to supply the family with basic needs. For example, in the rural area of Balochistan there is a shortage of drinking water. As a result, girls must fech water to supply the family. This situation means that levels of literacy and primary enrolment are the lowest in the entire country[39].

In Mexico, the rural and indigenous communities that cannot subsist on agricultural production, cattle raising, forestry or local handicrafts, are forced to migrate in family units, seeking seasonal jobs in agro-industrial companies. The employer pays a global sum for the work of the father, the mother and the children. Generally, it is the father who receives the payment, as he is considered the head of the family. By migrating, girls' and boys' attendance in school becomes totally irregular. Recently, the Education Project for Migrant Agricultural Day-workers has started to provide basic education to migrant girls, boys and adults, through a flexible strategy adapted to the needs of these groups.

In the E-9 countries, rural areas suffer from marginalisation. In the countryside there are few public health and education services and inadequate transport and communication. The large national educational enterprises of the 20th century did not fulfil all their objectives in the rural areas of these countries. In order to understand the magnitude of rural educational challenges, we must consider their remoteness and dispersion and the existence of linguistic minorities in countries such as Mexico, China and India.

In the last few years, awareness has grown of the need to formulate integrated development programmes for rural communities to guarantee the access of boys and girls in these areas to relevant and quality basic education.

Graph 8: Female literacy and child mortality[42] at the end of the nineties

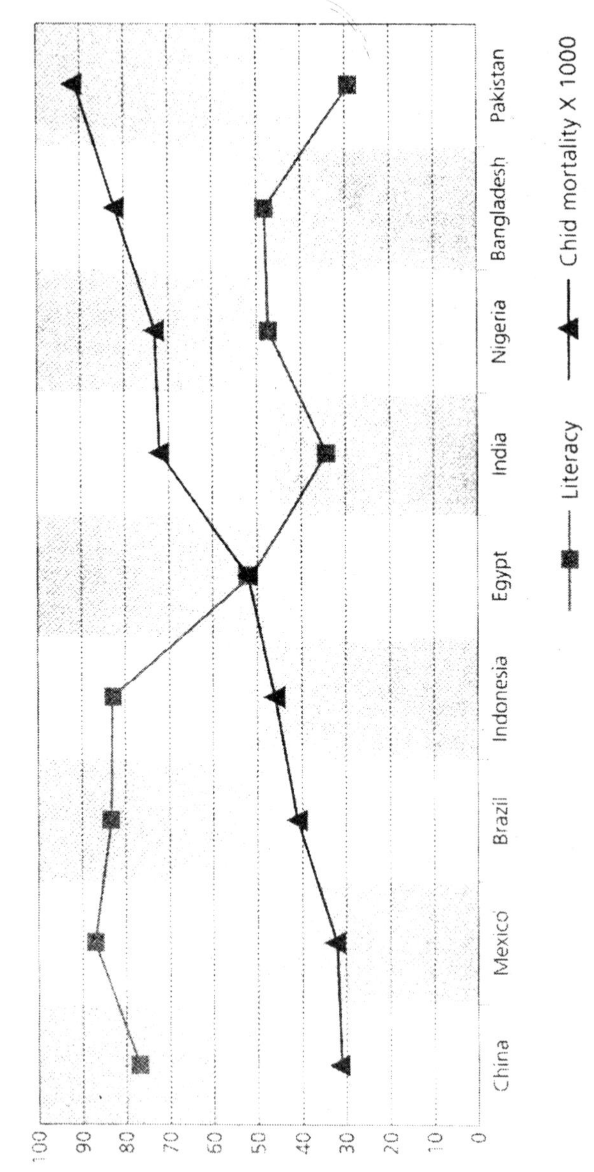

Source: National Reports on the EFA-2000 Assessment.

Graph 9: Variables classified according to GDP per capita[45] at the end of the nineties

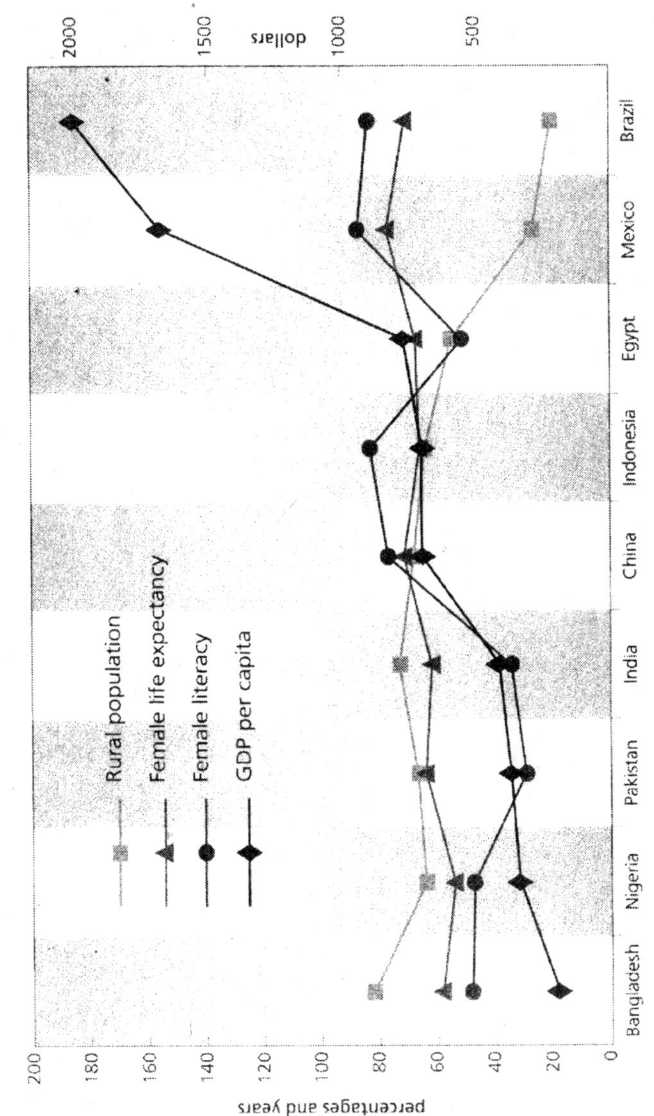

Source: National Reports on the EFA-2000 Assessment.

The two countries with relatively small rural populations (Brazil, with 20 per cent and Mexico, with 26.5 per cent) are those which have reached the highest rates of female literacy (83.2 per cent and 87.1 per cent, respectively)[40].

Indonesia has very high levels of female literacy (82.9 per cent) despite having a high rural population rate (64 per cent). It would be useful to make an in-depth evaluation of the educational coverage of girls and boys and of the adult literacy processes, and the action that made this relative success possible, especially the aspects that allowed it to offer relevant and good quality education in the rural environment.

THE RELATIONSHIP OF WOMEN'S LITERACY TO CHILD MORTALITY AND FERTILITY RATES

Several relevant socio-demographic indicators relating to female literacy will be analysed, that may throw some light on the importance of the education of women so they can help themselves and their children obtain a better standard of living.

In this section we start with the hypothesis that the higher the literacy rates and level of education of the mother, the lower the child mortality and fertility rates. It is clear that women with more education provide their children with greater possibilities of well-being. Education for pregnancy and for child-rearing should form an important part of the education agenda of E-9 countries.

The participation of the number of women in the total population of each country (graph 7) increases as the rural population falls and female literacy rises, as does the life expectancy of women at birth.

In order to evaluate this information we have to consider that globally, women form the absolute majority in the total population of each country. However, high female mortality rates and the related fall in life expectancy at birth is causing women to become an absolute minority in Pakistan and India.

It is important to note that the countries with the highest female literacy rates also have the lowest child mortality rates (as shown in graph 9). A useful task would be to identify whether the lack of proper preparation of mothers for childbirth and rearing their children is a cause of child mortality, compared to other variables such as the degree of development of public health systems.

Graph 10: Life expectancy, male and Female at the end of the nineties

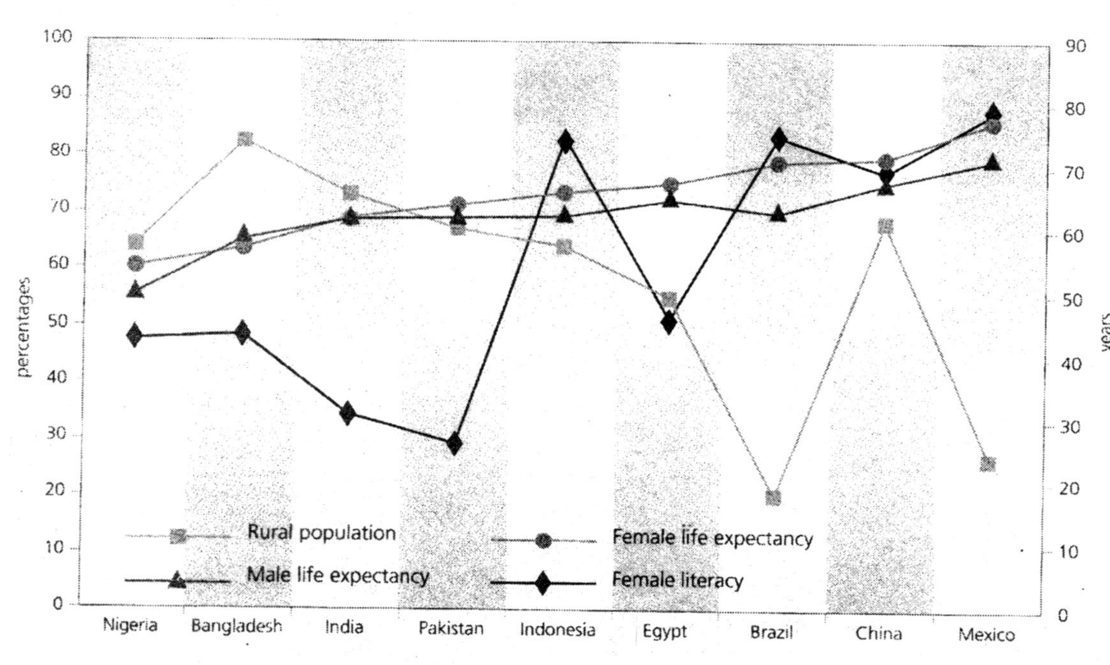

Source: National Reports on the EFA-2000 Assessment.

Graph 11: Male-Female literacy parity rate at the end of the nineties

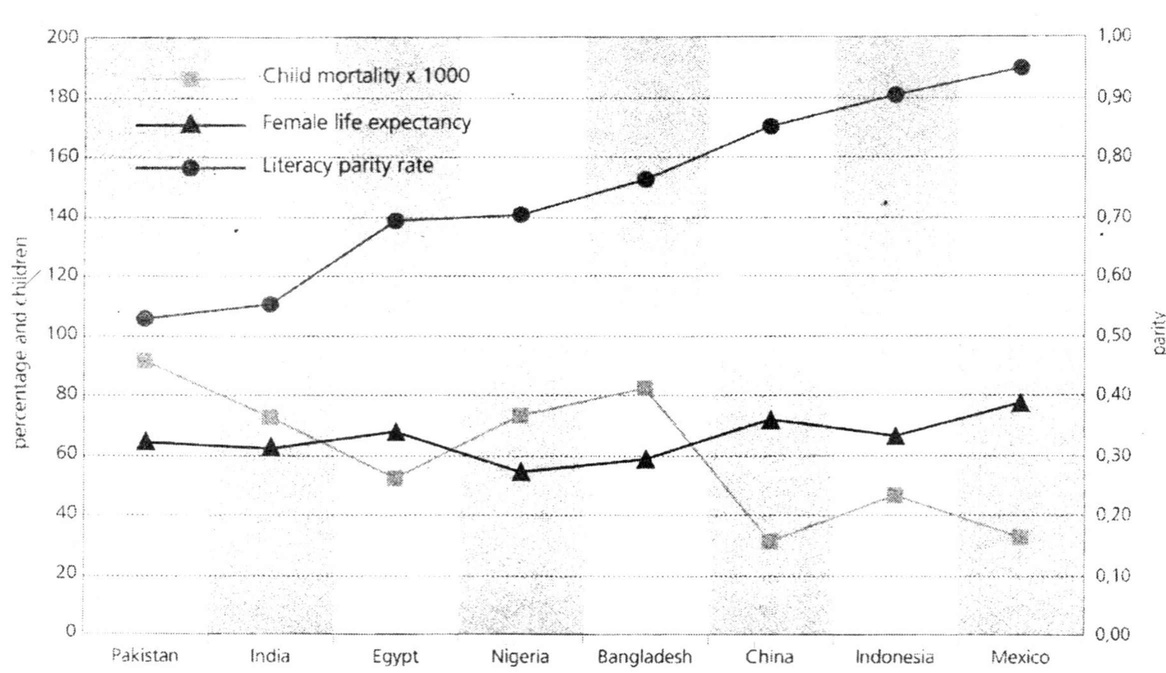

Graph 12: Literacy and life expectancy parity rates at the end of the nineties

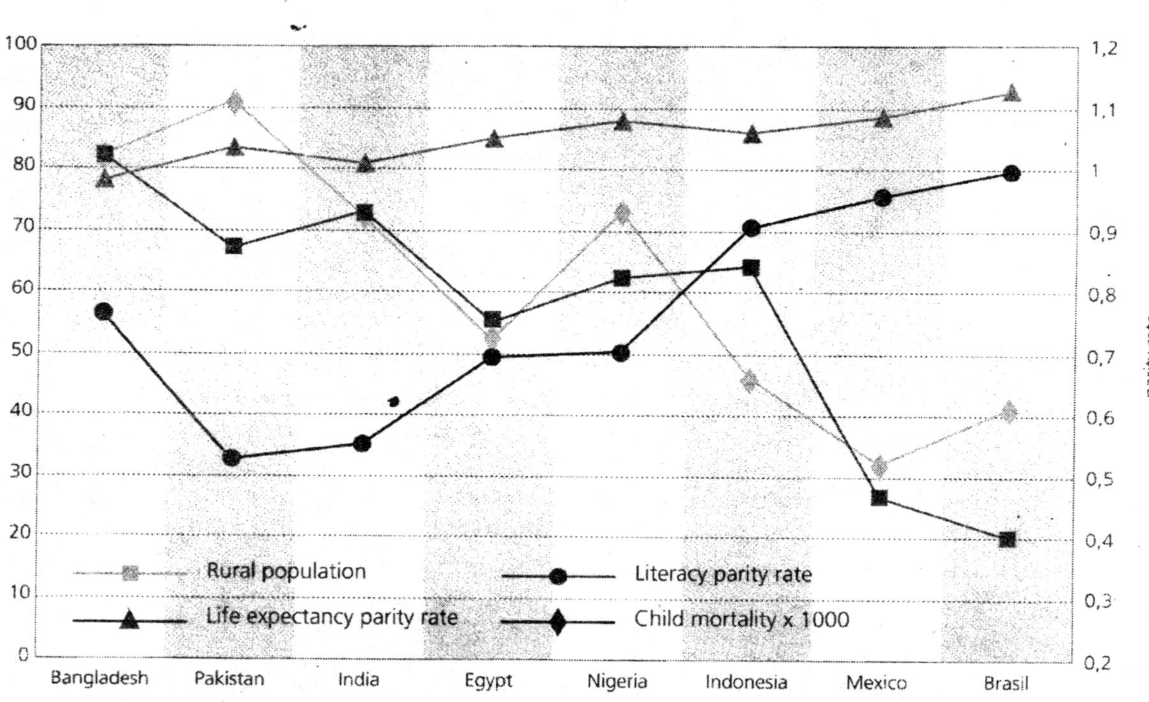

In Pakistan, the public sector provides the principal health services to the rural and urban population; however, most of the services are concentrated in urban areas where women have more information and the literacy rate is higher. The fertility and child mortality rates are therefore lower compared to rural areas.

Indonesia is perhaps the only country that deviates from this pattern. The level of female literacy is very high (82.9 per cent) and the child mortality rate is also high (71 per every 1000 live births)

A study carried out in Bangladesh[43] found that literate women received and applied health care information more efficiently, and that there was a positive relationship between the education of the mother and the health of their children, as well as to the child survival rate. A comparative study carried out in Malaysia, Bangladesh, Indonesia, India and Pakistan demonstrates that there is an inverse relationship between education and child mortality. In Bangladesh the number of surviving children rises with the increase in female literacy.

India, Nigeria, Bangladesh and Pakistan show the highest child morality rates and, at the same time, the lowest female literacy rates. In India, 87 per cent of children suffering form malnutrition have illiterate mothers. The same phenomenon occurs in Bangladesh[44]. A study from Nepal claims that "the average schooling of mothers whose children suffered from malnutrition was only 0.3 years, while the mothers of well-fed children had an average schooling of two years, this even though the fathers of the children with malnutrition problems had a higher level of schooling".

In Nigeria the life expectancy of women is only 54 years. Less than 50 per cent of women of reproductive age are aware of modern family planning methods and less than 4 per cent use contraception.

The highest levels of GDP per capita, considered as an indicator of the degree of wealth of societies, is found in those countries with the smallest rural populations and where literacy and life expectancy at birth of women are high. Greater participation and decision-making power of women in the formation and management of families and institutions is common in societies that participate in the production and global exchange of commercial and cultural goods and services[45].

As can be seen in graph 10, as female literacy falls and the rural population increases, the advantage of women over men in terms of life expectancy at birth declines, is eliminated and becomes a disadvantage in the case of Bangladesh.

Taking the male and female literacy rate, if the parity of the female indicator compared to the male is obtained, we have an approximation of the inequality in the educational development of the entire adult population, which depends on the history of the development of basic education in each country. As the parity approaches zero, it may be assumed that there is a greater shortfall in female education. In graph 11 the variables of child mortality, access to drinking water and life expectancy at birth of women are ordered according to the literacy levels by gender reached in each country.

With the exception of Nigeria, we can observe a clear tendency for the life expectancy of women to increase and child mortality to fall, as parity rises.

By comparing the development of parity in literacy with the parity in life expectancy at birth, a close relationship (see graph 12) appears. Advances in the equality of literacy between men and women are accompanied by an improvement in female survival compared to that of male. These simultaneous advances with the parity between the sexes are accompanied by a clear reduction in the rural population and child mortality.

In China there is a close relationship between the educational level of mothers and child health. Additionally, in this country it has been proven that 46.4 per cent of mothers who did not provide protein and vitamin supplements to children aged six months and over were illiterate or semi-illiterate. Among the mothers whose education went beyond 2 of secondary school, only 12.1 per cent did not add these supplement to their children's diets.

2

WOMEN AS EDUCATORS IN SCHOOLS

Education systems place great responsibility on both male and female teachers to educate, train and guarantee the attendance of boys and girls in school. It is therefore important to analyse the female schoolteachers' role to determine their influence on the education of girls.

Whatever the percentage of female teachers in a basic education system, it is necessary to value their role as educators, in order to offer them working conditions that lead to the development of girls and the community as a whole. It is a fact that the educational success of girls and boys depends to a great extent on the job satisfaction of teachers, their level of commitment and whether they get the moral and economic recognition they deverse.

The development of this section is based on two assumptions.

A) A higher rate of female participation in classroom teaching leads to higher rates of schooling and survival to the 5th grade of primary school, principally of girls.

B) The higher the proportion of rural populations, the lower the rates of access and survival of boys and girls in school.

THE IMPORTANCE OF WOMEN AS EDUCATORS IN SCHOOLS

Together with students, teachers are a central part of the school system. The efficiency of educational programmes greatly depends on the quality of the teachers.

A teacher is not just someone who stands up in front of group in order to give a lesson; he or she should treat the boys and girls with patience, affection and care, preparing them to work for a decent standard of living, as well as reinforcing social role models that promote gender equality.

Due to motherhood, and traditional family responsibilities, women are prepared to relate to children. This is undoubtedly a great advantage that facilitates teaching. However, it is not enough. Professional training is required so that women may perform optimally in education systems. In traditional societies it is also important for female teachers to give parents greater confidence in sending their daughters to school.

Despite the importance of this work, the teaching profession, especially as exercised by women in the first years of education, suffers from low status and low salaries. Mechanisms have to be found which allow the social re-evaluation and strengthening of the teaching profession in basic education, and raise the income of teachers. For example, in Mexico, the "Teaching Career" programme is a system of horizontal promotion that gives teachers the possibility of raising their wages, after enrolling in an evaluation of their performance as teachers and a training process. In this way, teachers do not have to be promoted in the administrative hierarchy or enter higher levels of education in order to advance professionally and obtain a higher income for a decent personal and family life. Female teachers benefit most as they account for the majority in basic education.

The number of women teachers is generally higher during the first stages of education. Such participation falls progressively at higher levels.

For example in Mexico, Brazil, China and Egypt, the percentage of female teachers is usually very high, above all in preschool. It seems to be common practice that women are in charge of boys and girls from 0 to 5 years old, which is understandable given that women have traditionally played this fundamental role in the family.

Several E-9 countries have stated their concern regarding the level of education of preschool teachers. The role of women as educators in school, as well as in the family, should not be reduced to intuition and traditional forms of child raising; they must be properly trained and prepared. Female teachers—from preschool on—should be given training and education so their work is not based solely on common sense, but on their knowledge. The professionalisation of the female education sector is very important in the development of E-9 countries.

In Brazil the situation of many female teachers in preschool centres gives concern, as they have no preparation[46]. In 1993, a survey made in Belo Horizonte of 189 educators in 139 nursery schools, who work under agreement with the Ministry of Social Development, showed that 2.7 per cent of these teachers were unpaid, 10.4 per cent earned less than monthly minimum wage, 54.2 per cent earned the minimum wage, and just 27.3 per cent earned more than the minimum wage. Studies made in various states of Brazil demonstrate that most women who teach in preschool education have not even completed their basic education. This proportion varies from state to state, from 12.2 per cent in Blumenau to 47.3 per cent in El Salvador[47]. In Brazil, the salaries paid to domestic help are similar to the salaries of preschool teachers almost all over the country, except perhaps for São Paulo, where they earn slightly more[48].

Regarding primary education, in Bangladesh the female teacher rate is 28 per cent, while in secondary education it is only 13.88 per cent[49]. Most female teachers are young and single. It is believed that women have natural skills that helps them to be good teachers. One study observed that "there is a direct correlation between employing women in education and the enrolment and attendance of girls in school"[50]. In fact, the 1991 Primary Education Act recommends that 60 per cent of teaching staff should women. However, achieving this is complicated by lack of teacher training. It is estimated that it will take more than 25 years to achieve this percentage. On the other hand, boys and girls are not permitted to mix; the curriculum is different for each sex, as is educational orientation regarding social roles. The same segregation happens in Pakistan, where priority is given to the attendance of boys in school.

Although girls must overcome many obstacles in attend school in India, the presence of female teachers seems to break these barriers, as will be seen further on. Until 1993, the rate of female teachers in primary school was 31 per cent, rising to 35 per cent in later grades. This situation usually varies when regional studies are made, with gender inequality becoming clear. In Bihar, a very vulnerable state, the rate of female teachers is 20 per cent, while in Kerala, the most advanced state in terms of education, it reaches 67 per cent. There is a great correlation between the female literacy rate in the states ad the size of the school populations that complete primary school[65]. In the states with greatest illiteracy there are fewer female teachers. For example, in the districts of Assam, Karnatka, Madhya Pradesh, Maharashtra and Orissa, less than a quarter of primary school teachers are women[51].

In India, 90 per cent of teachers are female i the field of special education. This high rate is related to the traditional idea that children with disabilities require care and attention that can only be provided by women.

In Egypt, women constitute 46.6 per cent of the total number of teachers, however, as in other countries, they form a majority in the first levels of education: 98.7 per cent in preschool; 96.4 per cent in one-classroom primary-schools; 52.2 per cent in primary schools; 42.8 per cent in preparatory schools; 36.6 per cent in general secondary schools; 34.4 per cent in technical secondary schools; and 28.5 per cent in agricultural secondary schools[52].

In 1993 many Egyptian female teachers were not graduates. For this reason, teacher training updating programmes were implemented, which have started to bear fruit. By 1997-98, 85.8 per cent of female primary school teachers had receive teacher-training courses. However, only 22.2 per cent of all female teachers had higher education.

Continuous teacher training is considered a major goal in Egypt. A comprehensive in-service training programme was organised by the Ministry of Education in co-ordination with several faculties of education to upgrade all elementary school teachers to university level. The programme was offered on a part-time basis and depended on distance learning and self-teaching strategies. Like Mexico, Egypt has developed a network of technological development centres for teacher training. As in many countries, both male and female teachers are sent abroad for training in the use of new technologies and teaching methods.

In Nigeria a similar problem exists regarding qualifications. In primary schools, in 1994, 50.34 per cent of female teachers qualified with Grade II Certificates, which are obtained after four years of lower secondary school, while only 39.9 per cent had higher grades (High School or West African School Certificate[53]). The training given to these teachers that same year lead to the National Education Certificate, normally awarded after three years' high school study. However, these teachers are not as well prepared to teach in secondary school as female university graduates[54].

The number of women teachers in Nigeria grew between 1984 and 1994. In primary education there were 104,024 female teachers while by 1994 there were 201,905; in secondary schools, in 1984 there were 29,902, while by 1994 there were 54,949. The arrival of women in the Nigerian school environment covers a shortage caused by the desertion of male teachers, who prefer to work in better-paid activities. However these national figures hide regional disparities. For example, in the southern states of Anambra and Lagos, which are more developed, there were 92 per cent and 80 per cent female primary school teachers, respectively, while in the poorer states of Sokoto and Jigawa, these numbers were 12.7 per cent and 4.7 per cent.

Female teachers serve as a model for girls for their own empowerment and provide them with advice and orientation for their personal life. However, they receive low wages, work in precarious conditions and lack educational materials. In fact this very situation is what has forced male teachers to seek other job horizons; the female teachers who have replaced them have only inherited the problem. Nigerian female teachers usually have other sources of income, such as selling goods inside and outside of school.

In Pakistan, despite policies to increase the number of female teachers in basic education, to allow greater schooling of girls, religious and socio-cultural factors prevent the achievement of this objective.

As can be seen in graph 13, the countries with the highest rural populations have the fewest female teachers. Countries with smaller rural populations, such as Mexico and Brazil, have a greater proportion of female teachers. In the context of the E-9 countries, levels of literacy in China and Indonesia are high if the size of the rural population is taken into account.

In China, female teachers who work in remote areas have been trained in their own communities and are familiar with local customs

Graph 13: Education and rural population[55] at the end of the nineties

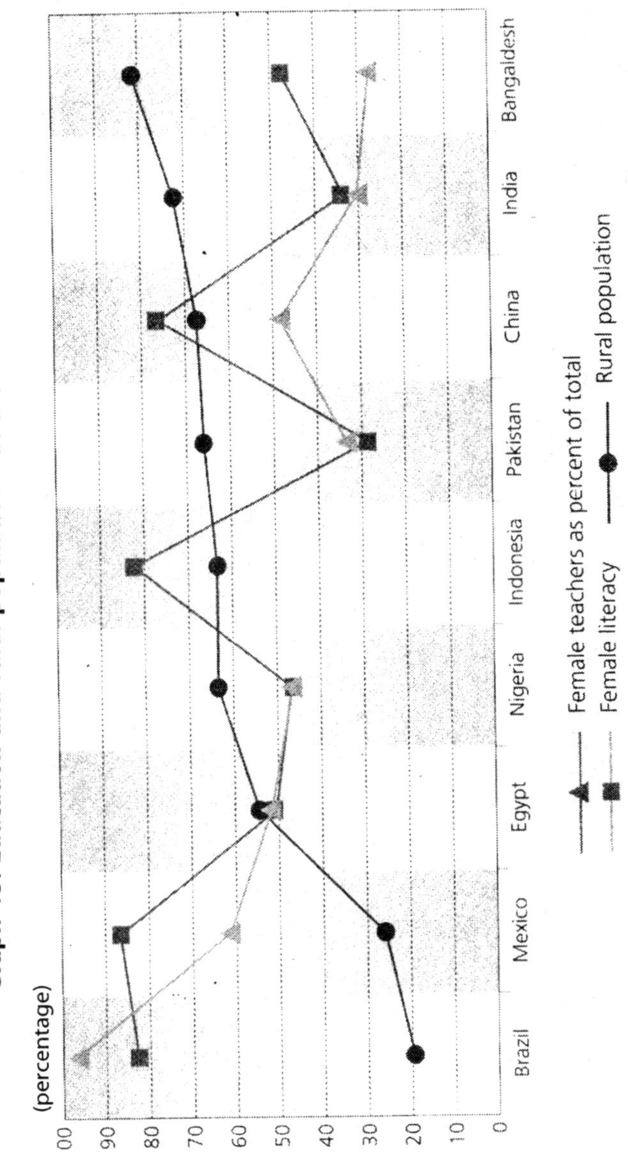

Source: Documents from countries and the UN, 1996

and realities. However, the number of well-trained women teachers in rural areas is very low. This is partly due to the fact that the infrastructure for training teachers in remote areas is insufficient and the potential candidates are unwilling or unable to travel to urban centres; on the other hand, trained women teachers do not want to be transferred to rural areas without transport or communication, where living conditions are precarious, health services are inadequate and there are no supplies, drinking water, or electricity[56].

Ningxia, a high-population Chinese province, is an example of the increase in the number of women teachers over the last few years. In 1992, the percentage of female primary school teachers in this province was 41.3 per cent, by 1997 the rate had risen to 45.2 per cent and in secondary schools it rose from 28.1 per cent to 36.3 per cent, a significant achievement[57].

Inequality between men and women, as well as inequality between urban and rural areas, are related to traditional preconceptions of the roles of women and men. In some cultures, it is still taboo for women to work outside their home, in any other way than attending to their family. However, a study on women discovered that their reasons for working as teachers are similar to those of men: to share knowledge and to be with young people. But it was also noted that women teachers were absent more frequently than their male counterparts due to the in many obligations and the double or triple shifts they had to work[58].

Another table (urban/rural, 1996) presented by Indonesia shows that 23 per cent of women teachers had not finished primary school, 37.2 per cent completed primary education, while only 2.9 per cent had a university degree. Men are also at an advantage, with 18 per cent not having completed primary school, 39.2 per cent having completed primary education, and 3.8 per cent having achieved some professional level of education[59].

The female population in Brazil is concentrated in preschool and the first grades of primary school, where they account for 97.4 per cent of the total. In the last years of primary school (from the fifth to eighth grades) 80.6 per cent of teachers are women and in secondary school, for the following three years, women occupy only 60.8 per cent of teaching jobs[60].

In Mexico, women represent 99 per cent, 62 per cent and 46 per cent of the total number of teachers in preschool, primary and secondary schools, respectively[61]. in Barzil, it has been verified that in the grades above basic education (fifth to eighth), there are fewer female teachers than in the lower grades (97.4 per cent in the first four years and 80.6 per cent in the last four years).

Several countries have confirmed that girls are very dedicated to their studies and when they get the opportunity to enter-school they are more tenacious, at least during the early years. However, when they reach secondary school, the number of girls gets smaller, as does the number of women teachers. It is precisely in these initial grades of secondary school where female teachers and mothers should support girls with a solid educational plan that allows them to continue to learn during their entire lifetime.

In a study of the regions of Mexio it emerged that in the poorest states with the largest indigenous populations, such as Chiapas (74 per cent) and Hidalgo (85 per cent), the percentage of women who do not go on to secondary education is much higher. Other determining factors are the level of education of the mother and the number of children she has, as well as the educational processes used in the school[62].

WOMEN'S PARTICIPATION IN DECISION-MAKING IN SCHOOLS

An essential factor for education systems is to give the schools greater autonomy. They can then determine a school project and the best forms of administration and management according to the social and environmental context. In general terms, this allows the school to ensure, along with the rest of the education system, that its service is relevant to different population groups. In some E-9 countries, such as Mexico, school autonomy is the last link in a process of decentralisation of education systems.

In E-9 countries, equal rights have been recognised for male and female teachers. However, the advances made along these lines are different. On the one hand, female participation in decision-making in education depends on the spaces created for women where decisions concerning school life, administration and management. On the other, the importance the school management gives to communication and co-ordination with parents and the community is an important factor.

Graph 14: Female net enrolment rate, female teachers and rural population at the end of the nineties

(percentage)

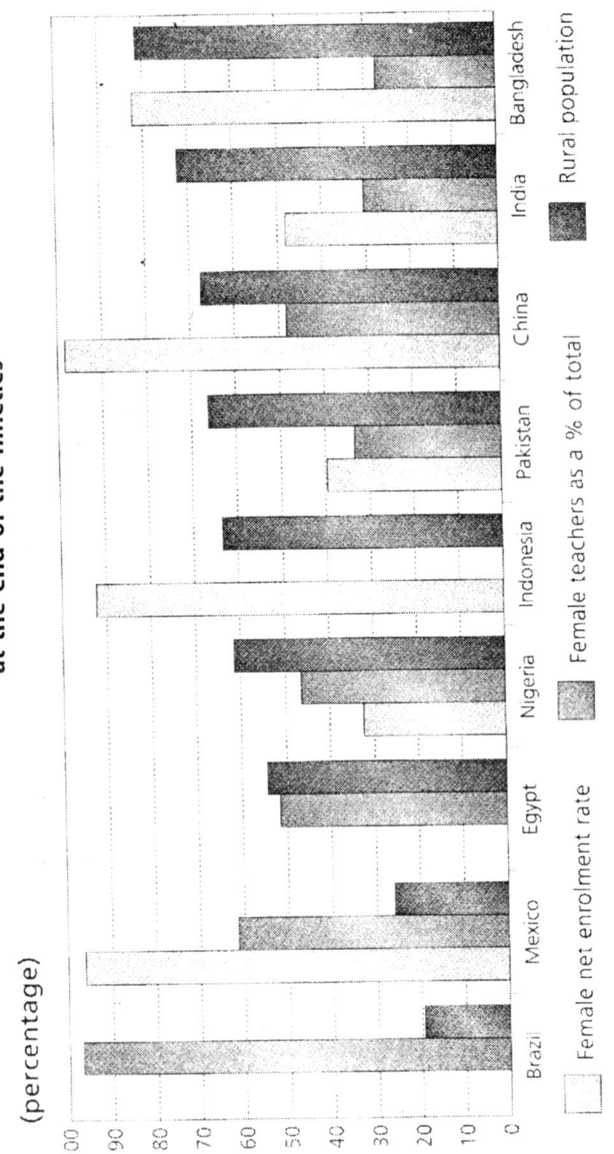

Source: Documents from countries and the UN, 1996

An improved participation of women in decision-making in schools is difficult to achieve if the education systems have not previously created the possibility for women to participate in important decisions.

Currently, access to the administrative or management structure is the only way in which male and female teachers can receive higher wages. In general, men are given access to these positions, motivated, to a large extent, by the need to take home the best possible income while benefiting from the conventions of society that give men greater management roles.

Therefore, it is important that the education systems should differentiate an administrative or management career from a teaching career, creating formulas that reward both good administrators and directors as well as good classroom teachers. Schools would greatly benefit from a structured system in which teachers purse their professional and economic development without neglecting their teaching vocation and specific skills. An example of how to achieve these objectives is the aforementioned *Teaching Career* programme carried out in Mexico.

In primary schools, two out of three school principals are men. But there are three women teachers for every two male, clearly indicating that men have better chances of obtaining management positions. The Mexican states with the lowest participation of female principles are Campeche (10.70 per cent female principals and 89.30 per cent male principals), and Zacatecas (18.32 per cent female principals and 81.68 per cent principals), and the ones where women are most favoured are the Federal District of Mexico City (the capital) (77.14 per cent female principals and 22.86 per cent male principals), and Baja California (56.13 per cent female principals and 43.87 per cent male principals).

In Brazil, educators who work in childcare centres are women from the same rural community who have not completed basic education or had any specific training. Both male and female teachers suffer from precarious working conditions in schools as well as low salaries. The inequity between genders is clearly manifested by the greater number of male teachers who teach in secondary and higher education, where better wages are offered[63].

Although exact figures are not available for all countries, Pakistan indicates tat in all the educational institutes for women, including district levels, the principals and managers are women.

WOMEN AS EDUCATORS IN RURAL SCHOOLS

In rural areas, girls and women have fewer opportunities for entering, remaining and completing basic education.

Even in countries with the highest national schooling and literacy indicators, where the rural population represents a very small percentage of the total population, certain regions present important challenges for basic education. In Mexico, for example, adult women over 40 who live in villages with less than 100 inhabitants are disadvantaged by an illiteracy rate of 50 per cent, while the national rate of literacy for adults is 12.9 per cent (see graph 15).

Notwithstanding the general trend, China emerges from this analysis as a special case. Even in rural contexts, girls are able to remain for several years in education. In 1996, general enrolment in secondary education reached 53,630,000 students with a dropout rate of 2.68 per cent. The female secondary school graduation rate in 1997 was 92.2 per cent. This data indicates that, in spite of having a rural population even bigger than Nigeria, Indonesia, Egypt and Pakistan, China has been able to develop significant strategies for the access and retention of girls in school.

As for the girls' enrolment rate among countries with the largest rural populations, Bangladesh seems to have made the most advances, after China. This also seems to be the case of Egypt, although this country presents a high net enrolment rate of 91.8 per cent.

Another fundamental issue is the presence of women teachers, above all in rural areas, so that girls remain in school. To this end, in Pakistan, China, Egypt, and Nigeria it is considered important to promote women as educators not only because they keep girls in school and help them perform better, but also to improve enrolment in both primary and secondary schools. All three countries are promoting the training of female teachers and their insertion in rural schools.

Unfortunately, in the rural environment many obstacles need to be overcome for female teachers to reach levels of professionalism and recognition. For example, in Pakistan, where most of the population

Graph 15: Mexican Republic illiteracy according to size of communities, age groups and gender

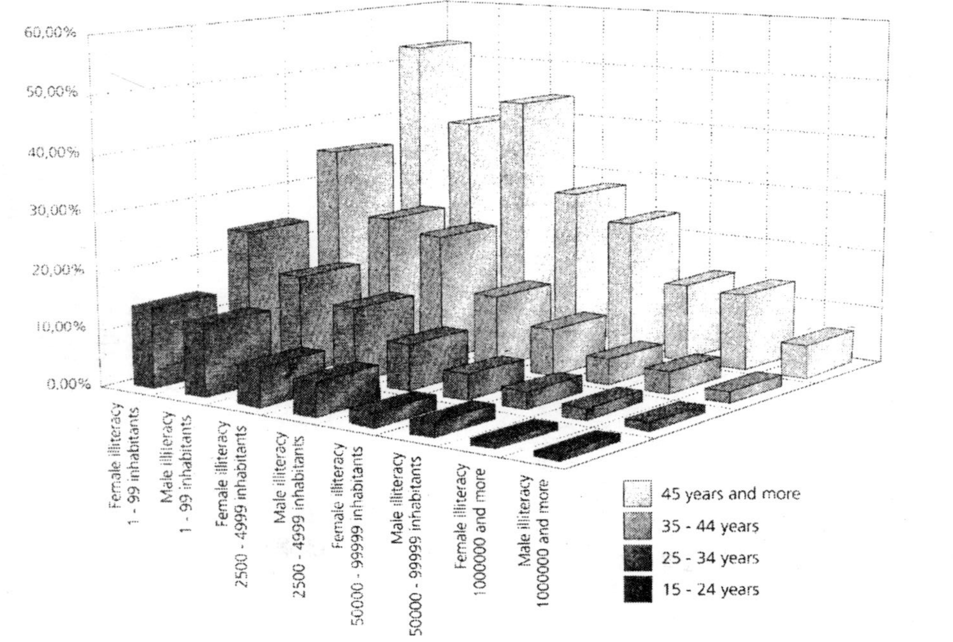

Source: Population and housing survey, 1995

lives in rural areas (66.7 per cent), there are fewer women teachers, as they are unwilling to go to remote places. Furthermore, most untrained female Pakistani teachers are in rural areas (¼ of the total). The problem is basically cultural. It is not socially accepted that women in rural areas go to work, which keeps female unemployment high. Nevertheless, as in India and Egypt, parents prefer to send their daughters to schools with women teachers. In the remote rural areas, not reached by women teachers, the adverse effects on the educational development of girls are reflected by low school enrolment and high illiteracy rates among women[64].

In Egypt's community schools, teachers or facilitators are recruited from the school's immediate community, so they do not have transport or housing problems. In addition, they know their students and their families very well, and can involve parents in educational decisions.

In India it has been demonstrated that parents, forced to send their daughters to distant schools, prefer female teachers. A study carried out in a primary school in Patini, district of Saharanpur, revealed that the inhabitants of very poor communities will send their sons and daughters to schools outside of their villages when the teachers are women, especially if they are from community. Nevertheless, the cultural impediments for the education of women are still enormous[65].

In some poor areas in China, girls have little access to primary school. This is partly due to the shortage of female teachers in these environments. Although the impact of a larger number of women teachers on the female enrolment has not been properly analysed, there are anecdotes that confirm its positive influence. Contrary to what happens in Pakistan and Nigeria, female teachers are very well received in the most marginalised areas. In local people's eyes, they are symbols of wisdom.

A study carried out in three schools in Ningxia (in China) demonstrated that by increasing the number of school principals, the number of female teachers also rose, from 36.1 per cent to 46.5 per cent. As a consequence, the enrolment of girls in primary school rose from 71.2 per cent to 97 per cent. The presence of women teachers reduces the concern of parents regarding the safety and moral values of their daughters and encourages them to participate[66]. It is important to continue supporting the training of rural women teachers, preferably from the local community, in order to promote trust and confidence among parents.

3

WOMEN AS EDUCATORS IN THE COMMUNITY

Several recent studies have shown that women play an important role in the transformation of societies, as well as in the transmission of values and attitudes in the community. In many cases they facilitate access to goods and services indispensable for community life. But women not only transform the social structures of the community, they also play an important role in the transmission of the collective memory and in the recreation of cultural codes that contribute to the group's identity.

A community is a collective group that transcends the family and establishes bonds based on interests such as territoriality, relationships, friendship, social interests, values or the economy. Communities are groups in which people congregate to organise their personal, family and social life.

Women play an important educational role in the community, because they are responsible for educating their children. Women also exercise an influence over the rest of the community in order to guarantee their integrity and development.

This chapter describes the different roles that women have adopted in the community to improve living conditions, as well as transmitting values and norms. A comparison will be made between the E-9 countries of the current functions women perform as educators in daily life, especially in the rural environment.

THE ROLE OF WOMAN IN THE COMMUNITY

The role that women play in the communities of the different countries is related to the traditions, values, customs and morality of the inhabitants. What seems to vary from country to country is the type of relationship established in each case. In the most traditional societies, with a high rural population rate, such as Bangladesh, India Egypt, Pakistan, Nigeria, Indonesia and China, the role of women is to transmit the customs and rules followed in the communities for years. In China, Women who live in cities seem to have reached a different status. However, the disparity between rural and urban areas is very evident: some regions reach the standard of living of developed countries, while others are below the average of developing countries.

In Mexico and Brazil, countries with a low rural population rate, women play diverse roles in the community. Those who live in urban and marginalised urban areas are powerful agents for change, as they actively participate in public and social life. Women in the marginalised areas of Brazil organise themselves in order to define their role in relation to public institutions. Their attempt to achieve interaction extends democratic areas for participation and decision-making, incorporating the community in the management of schools with the possibility of being involved in their administration.

In indigenous rural areas, in Mexico, women have little influence in terms of generating change. The same thing occurs in the rural areas of Brazil, where Afro-American women are particularly disfavoured: the highest illiteracy rate in the country is found among women over 40 in this group[67]

In the rural areas of Brazil, the average monthly income of families is less than half of those in urban areas. Most rural families are headed by men, whose average level of educaiton corresponds to half the urban average (5.5 years of study in cities and 2.2 in the country).

This unfavourable situation has lead rural workers (both male and female) to organise themselves in order to obtain better standards of living. One of the most important organisations in this country is the Landless Movement (Movimiento de los Sin Tierra—MST), which has modernised work relations as well as gender relations. In this movement the male hierarchy has been questioned. The movement's settlements allow families to totally break away from daily life and live in a community, sharing tasks, irrespective of the roles traditionally more attributed to the sexes[68]. Men, women, girls and boys participate in tasks such as cooking, agricultural production, security, cleaning, and childcare, contrary to the norm.

Starting with their fight for union rights, women organised themselves and created the Women's Movement. This altered patriarcal relations in the rural family, as it implied the mobilisation of women, their participation in public life and in activities outside of the family circle, as well as a certain abandonment of domestic chores[69].

In Mexico, the indigenous peoples adhere strongly to traditional values. Women receive and transmit knowledge and attitudes regarding society and life, moulded according to what their culture considers as male and female behaviour. Girls, either by imitation, observation or education, learn to carry out all the activities that will fulfill the expectations that others have of them.

There are currently approximately 10 million[70] indigenous people in Mexico, who speak more than 80 languages and dialects. They form 64 ethnic groups with their own traditions, language and culture. In Mexico efforts have been made to include the indigenous population while respecting their cultural diversity. A bilingual-intercultural education system has thus been created, which reinforces their culture and traditions and also extends knowledge of Spanish, the country's official language. In 1999-2000 school year it is estimated that 288,400 and 789,000 boys and girls attended indigenous preschool and primary schools.

An important activity to strengthen the educaiton of indigenous mothers is initial education, which consists of providing mothers and fathers with orientation regarding healthcare, diet and education of their sons and daughters. However, inequality regarding ethnic, rural and gender status become evident when regional studies are made. The states of Chiapas, Oaxaca, Hidalgo and Guerrero, with the largest indigenous populations, are the poorest in the country. The highest rate of illiteracy is among indigenous women.

Together with Mexico and Brazil, China is one of the most advanced E-9 countries in terms of women's empowerment. In urban areas, women work and receive payment. In China, however, equality is difficult due to the existence of a large number of different nationalities (56), that complicate the task of education. The Han nationality is the most extensive, accounting for 90 per cent of the population. Six of the minorities have high levels of education, even above the level of national development.

In Pakistan, India, Egypt, Indonesia, Bangladesh and Nigeria, countries in which the majority of the population belongs to traditional cultures, women are starting to mobilise in favour of their own empowerment in Indonesia, rural women form the most disadvantaged group of the population. The lack of opportunities for mothers to study and develop in other fields means that girls reproduce traditional patterns.

A similar occurs in Pakistani traditional society where religion and ancestral values provide the framework of community life. In Pakistan, a somewhat feudal and tribal structure remains. The culture favours men, their education and their future. In the community, education encourages women to continue to play their role as mothers and wives; however, productive and community work is required from them. Pakistani women are currently assuming an active role as agents of educational development in their communities. This role is multifaceted and varied. Numerous organisations have recently appeared to support the functions of women in communities. One of the most important organisations is the All Pakistan Women's Association, which includes the intelligent participation of Pakistani women in the country's development among its objectives.

In Bangladesh community work is divided in two: it consist of voluntary work generally performed by women, assuring the provision and maintenance of resources such as healthcare, education and water supply; and community administration, which refers to politics and is principally carried out by men in the formal political environment. The latter (unlike the women's work), is generally paid work that confers both power and status. Women's work goes mostly unnoticed and is poorly paid, in the best of cases. Wome in the rural environment are generally responsible for acquiring goods for family subsistence, cultivating and educating their children. Women handover the food or any other product made at home to their husbands so that they may go to market to sell them. Bangladeshi women play a fundamental role in agriculture, but only within the confines of the home. For this reason their work is not recorded in statistics, although it is no less important than that performed by men.

Over the last few years the panorama in Bangladesh has been changing. People now achnowledge that the participation of women in development programmes is fundamental for sustainable progress. Recently, more and more women have been contributing financially to the family, just like the men, and contributing to the eudcation of their sons and daughters. Studies show that the gains obtained by women through credit or in jobs benefit their children to a great extent: access to better health, school education, clothing and other benefits[71].

In Nigeria, the role of women as educators in the community is very important. In many Nigerian communities, the educational function of the family is transferred to the community. Adolescents are divided into age groups (10-13, 13.16, and 16-20) and initiated in their work. During this time, the society establishes duties and skills to be developed, as well as patterns of behaviour that the adolescents should observe. Some Nigerian communities still have initiation rituals, like the Efik community in the South East of Nigeria, whose ceremony known as "mbpo" prepares the community's young men for marriage. Among the Igbo, women carry out a ceremony called "iru mgbede", which includes a three-month period of preparation for marriage. During this time the mothers and other women from the community feed young girls and train them in nutrition, hygiene, beauty, marital duties, fertility and pregnancy.

In Egypt, women are gradually becoming a powerful agent of change and social development. Rural women have an important role to play within the family and the community: cultivating land, cattle and poultry raising, undertaking home-based tasks and managing small income-generating projects. However, in a survey carried out on the importance of education, 98 per cent of the people surveyed in three provinces said the educaiton of boys is important, while only 30 per cent said the same regarding girls. The prevalence of men completing university education is much greater than that of women.

In urban areas, Egyptian women play a significant role as educators in the community: they participate in social and educational projects through NGOs and other women's committees, and do voluntary work to improve the standard of living in their local communities.

Graph 16: Population growth

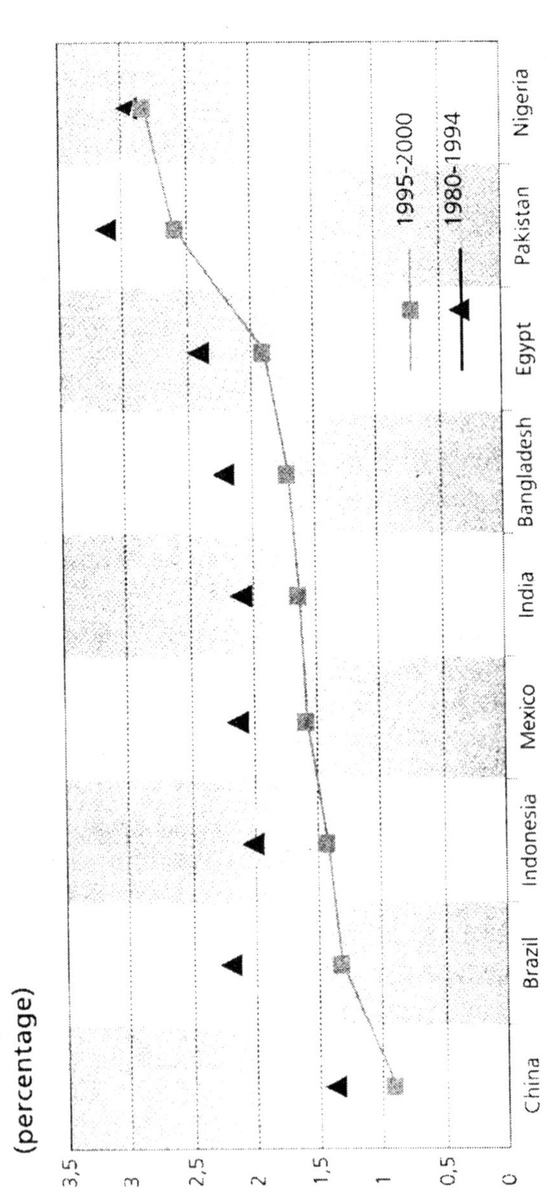

Source: UNESCO

In **India,** women have been disadvantaged compared to men in terms of social roles, access to education and personal development. Their participation in society has been limited, as they must comply with the rules considered appropriate for their sex. However, gender inequality was not so evident in India's distant past, when women were disciples of philosophy and theology, although the code of ethics made their place clear with the epithet: "shadharmini" (companion in the dharma).

Since the early 20th century, women in India have had a slightly different status. Between 1921 and 1947, the number of women who received education rose from 1.28 to 4.28 million. In some states and towns, inequality is evident. A study showed that in the town of Panalpur, the difference between castes caused variations in female literacy. There are still enormous inter-and intra-regional differences that have important implications for education policies.

Aspects of Indian culture also constitute an obstacle to the promotion of women's and girls' education; since marriage, Indian women have to go and live in their husband's village, their parents cannot see the benefits of dedicating time and resources on their education.

Although it is a traditional society, India's rich and diverse past can inspire a more positive role for women based on their education. In today's India there is a significant percentage of female teachers, "anganwadi" workers and health workers. These functions are the basis of rural management, from which a new vision of women in India can start to be built.

POPULATION GROWTH AND THE EDUCATION OF WOMEN

Explicit cultural obstacles to women's education and empowerment are directly related to the notion that women should only reproduce and care for their children.

Consequently a low percentage of women utilise modern contraceptive methods and are willing to give birth to the number of children that is physically possible. Although a lot has been achieved in the face of alarming forecasts for the nineties, population growth rates in 1994 remain high in E-9 countries. this is evident above ail in Nigeria and Pakistan, where no significant advance has been made.

Graph 17: Female education at the end of the nineties

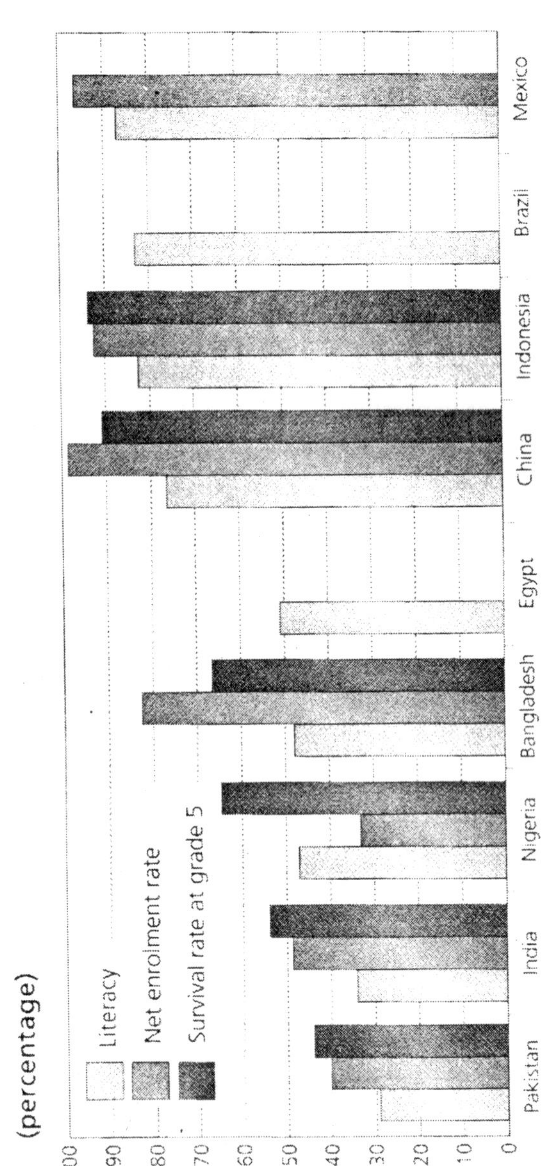

Source: National Reports on the EFA-2000 Assessment

In China, Brazil, India and Bangladesh, population growth rates have been lowered, against all expectations. The graphs 17, 18 and 19, which contain the population growth rate and literacy rates, net enrolment rate and 5th grade survival rate, show that there is a direct relationship between a fall in population growth and education, with certain variations. Although China has advances to make in women's literacy, it has the lowest population growt rate and the highest enrolment rates.

Pakistan has the lowest female literacy rate and the second highest population growth rate; additionally, the enrolment rate is also very low.

Recent research has confirmed that an increase in primary school enrolment generally precedes, an increase in literacy rates[72], by two years, which is cause for optimism in E-9 countries.

As can be seen in graph 18, the inverse relatioship between female literacy and population growth rates is very clear.

Gender inequality is shown when the graphs are broken down and male and female rates are compared. Female literacy, as can be seen in graph 19, is much lower than male literacy in all countries, except for Brazil where the difference is insignificant.

Population growth rates are not only related to literacy, but also to important factors such as reproductive health education. In Nigeria, a traditional and diverse society with a large rural population of (62 per cent) (see graph 20) and 250 ethnic-linguistic groups[73], a literacy programme per se would not suffice. Rather, an integrated literacy and reproductive health strategy must be implemented. Cultural resistance to change in Nigerian communities is also strong. For them, traditional education is no less important than what they call "western education" and they greatly value their traditions and customs. Women may be literate, but they might not be convinced that population growth is a problem.

Even with a large rural population and a low female literacy rate Bangladesh has a population growth rate lower than Pakistan, India, Egypt and Nigeria. Nevertheless, population growth and fertility rates indicate a very different situation. Although exact information was not provided in the document on Banladesh, it was indicated that men are opposed to constraceptive methods. Couples frequently reach an

Graph 18: Female literacy and population growth rates

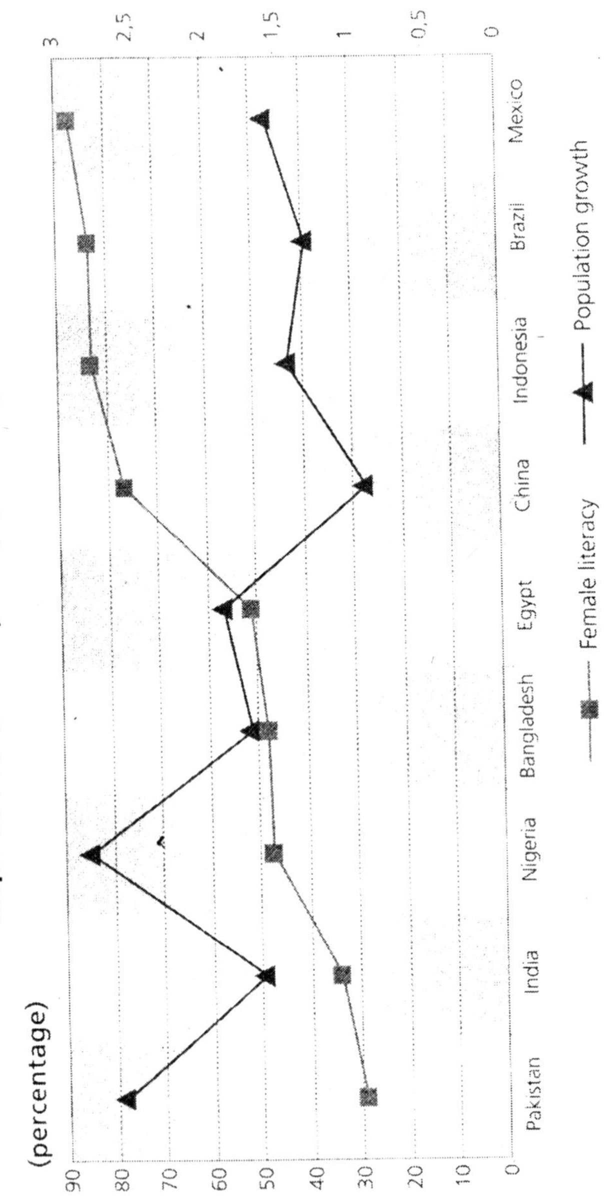

Source: National Reports on the EFA-2000 Assessment

Graph 19: Male and Female literacy at the end of the nineties

(percentage)

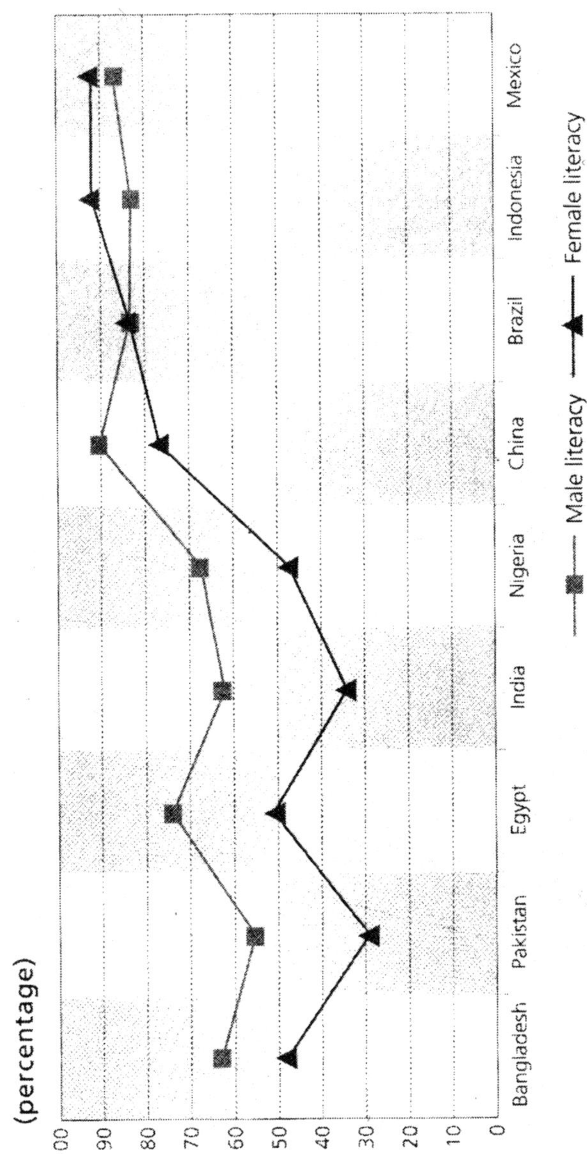

Source: National Reports on the EFA-2000 Assessment

agreement regarding the number of children they want to have and there are fewer families in which the man decides. It would be convenient to make an in-depth study, as the rural population rate is the highest in the E-9 countries (82 per cent); while, the population growth rate is declining.

This situation is possibly related to the fact that schooling levels in this country are higher than in Pakistan, India and Nigeria.

China and Indonesia have high female literacy rates, as well as low population growth rates, although they have large rural populations. Regarding Indonesia, the growth rate is one of the lowest, although the rural population is high (62 per cent).

China has made substantial advances towards the goals of abolishing illiteracy in general and female illiteracy specifically, as well as raising retention rates in primary school; however, in a regional revision, disparities between urban and rural areas and gender inequality become evident. In some provinces, for example Tibet, there is a school dropout rate of 5.02 per cent, in general, and 6.80 per cent for girls, one of the highest rates in the whole country. This rate contrasts with the national rate for girl primary school dropouts, which reaches only 0.92 per cent.

Notwithstanding the high rural population rate, this country has the lowest fertility rate and a high 5th grade survival rate. In depth studies would have to be made to confirm that hypothesis: China's regional development policies could be cited as an example of good practice benefiting the rural environment, and especially women.

In Nigeria and Pakistan, social development policies (including education) seem to have come across problems of access and dispersion of rural populations. If the analysis were to be based solely on these two countries, the hypothesis would be satisfactorily fulfilled: they have large rural populations, high fertility rates and low literacy and girls enrolment rates. We should take into account in all cases that the information on the 5th grade survival rate is partial in terms of giving a complete view of the state of education for girls, as no data on dropouts and repetition is available that would complete the reading.

Indonesia seems to have made the greatest advances in terms of gender equality. The female literacy rate is one of the highest, as is the enrolment rate and the 5th grade survival rate, and the fertility

Graph 20: Fertility rate at the end of the nineties

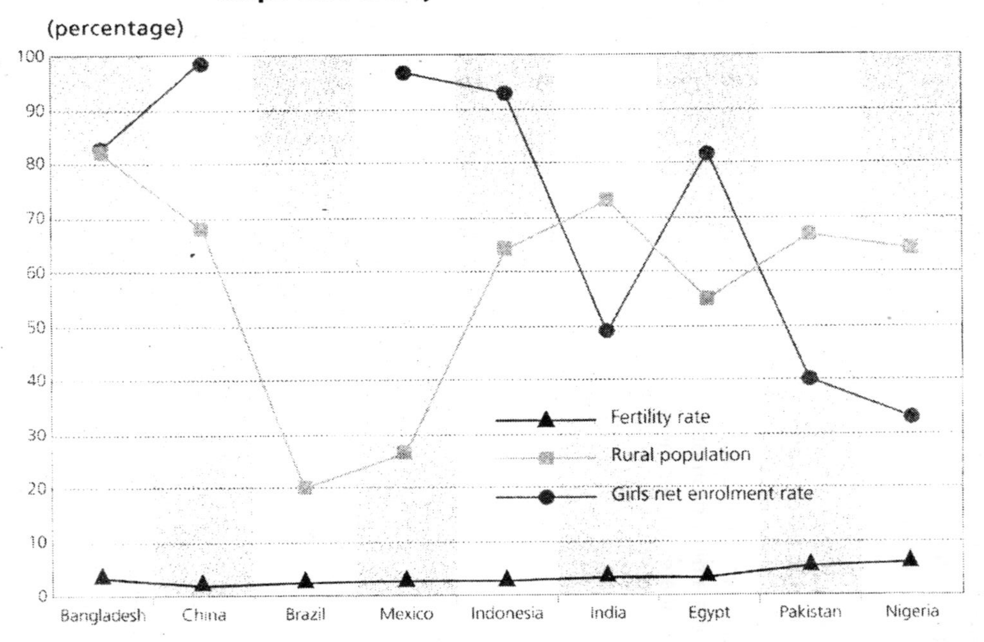

Source: National Reports on the EFA-2000 Assessment

rate is even lower than that of Mexico, a country with a high women's literacy rate, low rural population rate and high girls' enrolment.

It is a fact that in Indonesia women play a central role as educators in the community. Though only education and the transmission of values from mothers to daughters has been examined, women also dynamize communities by requesting specific services or creating alternatives for solving problems of survival. They work invisibly for health, food and the general well-being of the family.

Therefore, community education must be encouraged as it lays the bases for the development of social projects for certain groups. As community education is an interpersonal rather than a mass interaction, whose code of ethics corresponds to a specific group, it is a priority to develop community programmes for women's education, with the aim of promoting the education of girls and building codes to eliminate gender inequality.

4

WOMEN AS EDUCATORS IN PUBLIC LIFE

Women who work in the public environment continue to exercise their role as educators. Officials, businesswomen, politicians, spiritual leaders, university researchers, artists, are important role models for women in families and communities. These women, motivate other women with their exemplary professional performance and can alter their expectations from life and open up possibilities for decision-making, even if only in their own homes.

Involvement of women in public life is an element that transforms the status of women, as well as family relationships, the socialisation of children and the organisation and division of work.

The presence of women in the public arena has profound effects on traditional practices, attitudes and values based on a rigid division of work along gender lines and on stereotypes derived from this division.

This chapter will analyse different forms of participation of women in public life in E-9 countries. A section is included which mentions the national policies that have helped women take power and which greatly affect national life in both local and national political systems. The assumption is that higher levels of educational development of girls lead to higher rates of gender empowerment.

WOMEN'S EMPOWERMENT

In E-9 countries women's empowerment[74] is a relatively recent occurrence. Empowerment of women is understood to mean the self-determination and self-confidence that allows women to play an active role in society. In this section, women's empowerment in each country will be compared on the basis of the country studies.

China, Mexico, Brazil and Indonesia have the highest rates of income contributed by women.This reading is related to facts explained in other chapters, regarding the high levels of female literacy and net primary schooling for girls.China presents the highest rate of women's income. Indonesia stands out due to its high female literacy rate and girls' enrolment rate.

With the data on income earned by women, it can be seen that Indonesia is placed after China and before Mexico and Brazil, countries that have a better place in terms of gender empowerment measures (GEM)[75] and the Human Development Index[76], and a higher female literacy rate.Mexico occupies last place of these four countries in terms of women's income with Brazil in third place; however, the latter countries have a large percentage of women working in different sectors, except government. The highest gender empowerment measures are found among these countries. China has the highest, followed by Mexico, then Brazil and finally Indonesia.

The last place is occupied by Nigeria and Pakistan, which only confirms the trends already remarked in previous chapters. Both countries present disadvantages in terms of the empowerment of women.India, Egypt and Bangladesh follow.Out of these five countries, Bangladesh has the greatest empowerment measures and the second lowest female literacy rate, although its girls enrolment rate is high.

If the specific data included in the country studies are taken into account, the analysis can be complemented and enriched. With regards to the Human Development Index (HDI),China occupied 106th place out of 174 countries on the world in 1998. However, in terms of GEM, China occupied 33rd place, being placed even above Japan (38th), which is a reflection of the effort being made by this country to guarantee rights and empowerment for women.

Although the above does not indicate the number of women who participate in political life, complementary information on this topic is available. In 1997, 650 female congresswomen attended the 9th People's National Congress (PNC), representing 21.81 per cent of the total, which is a very high percentage, relatively speaking. The number of women on the Permanent Committee of the PNC rose from 14 in 1985 to 16 at present, with percentages of 9 and 11.85 per cent respectively. Two of the women were elected vice-chairwomen, corresponding to 10.5 percent of the total. The congresswomen of the PNC actively participate in decision-making. They have proposed valuable measures to the government to safeguard the interests and rights of women. The State Council has a woman member and the number of female ministers and vice-ministers has increased from 12 in 1985, to 17 present; i.e., from 5.2 to 6.6 per cent.

Although local government in China is at a disadvantage compared to the federal or central government, there is a considerable increase in the involvement of women in this environment. Locally, the number of female governors and vice-governors from 9 to 17 i.e., from 5 per cent to 12.26 per cent, in 1993. At present 23 provinces, 244 prefectures and 2,106 districts have women in the party or in local government. Assuming that greater participation of women in local polities will lead to a more rapid and efficient female empowerment process, then the case of China will have to be examined. The country is making important progress in its provinces, although it still shows shortfalls, above all in Muslim areas[77] and in the region of Tibet[78].

Following the aforementioned data regarding rural population, and the consequent marginalisation of women in this environment, it may be inferred that rural women are mostly found in occupations in which they do not exercise their decision-making power. 5.53 per cent are professionals; 0.45 per cent work in the government, 0.98 per cent are employees; 3.12 per cent work in business, 2.75 per cent in services; 75.26 per cent in agriculture, forestry, fishing and animal care, and 12.03 per cent in transport and industry. Most women work in agriculture and forestry and less than 10 per cent are government employees, businesspersons and professionals.

Gender inequality in China can also be seen when analysing a specific occupation, as in the case of medicine. In this country there are more women doctors than men and they share top positions with their male colleagues; however, the distribution is still unequal. Women progress more slowly and there are fewer women in administrative and decision-making positions. It is still very difficult in China for women to acquire top jobs[79].

In Mexico the number of women in Congress has increased considerably over the last few years. However, at the local level, inequality becomes clear. Women have much more possibilities in central and federal powers than in local powers. It is still difficult for people in the states to accept women in public environments.

Important advances have been made in Congress. The LIV and LV legislatures of the Mexican House of Congress in the period from 1988 to 1994 had a female participation of 12.5 per cent and 6.3 per cent, respectively. For the period 1994-2000, in the LVI and LVII legislatures, female participation was 11.7 per cent and 5.5 per cent. With regards to the Senate, Mexico City has an equal representation between women (5) and men (6). But out of 12 Mexican states there is only one women senator, and in three states there are only two female senators. There is no female representation in the rest of the country's states.

Maxican women have also occupied government positions. There have been three female governors, five secretaries of state and nine ambassadors. In late 1998, the rate of female official in middle-ranking and high-ranking positions in federal government, was 27 per cent. 11.8 per cent secretaries of state were women and on the level of junior ministers and civil servants, one in four jobs were held by women.

In local government, women are also a minority. Of the total number of officials in municipalities in 1998, only 12 per cent were women. Female representation in municipal governments is even smaller, barely 3.5 per cent. It should be underlined that the municipalities governed by women are small, with few inhabitants, and located in rural and marginalised areas.

In Mexico, as in Brazil[80], women play a very active role in an urban setting. In Brazil, in marginalised urban areas, women participate in processes of a wide range to claim and exercise their rights. Similarly, in Mexico, women are playing more active roles in solving the problems of their community and planning better social environments[81]. In both countries, women participate in organised civil society: in pro-human rights, community management, sexual and reproductive rights groups, environmentalist groups, groups for children with disabilities, among many others. In Mexico, the presence of women is evident in non-institutional politics and in social movements, on a local scale.

Regarding the Judiciary in Mexico, of the 11 members of the Supreme Court of Justice, only one is a woman, but women represent 19 per cent of all top jobs in this field, constituting one of the three powers where their presence is most significant.

Additionally, women have a strong presence in the political parties. Women were named as the first two National Presidents of two different political parties of Mexico in recent years.

In Nigeria, the Gender Development Index (GDI)[82] and the Gender Empowerment Measure (GEM) are very low. The first is 0.383, putting the country in 100th place out of 130 countries, and the second 0.196m 108th place out of 116 countries. The Human Development Index (HDI) is 0.406, occupying 141st place out of 172 countries[83]. In India, the GDI is 0.410 and the GEM is only slightly higher than that of Nigeria, 0.215. In both countries, judging by their indicators, gender empowerment is still very low.

In Bangladesh, the government has decided to reserve three seats on each local congress for the direct participation of women in the electoral process. In the last election, nearly 45,000 women competed for 14,000 seats and for first time they were elected as the people's representatives[84]. This has transformed the political structures and institutions that reinforced and perpetuated gender inequality. This opening has challenged a basic power relationship in this country. Now women have to negotiate with men, members of the Local Congress (Union Parishad), with the same resonsibilities and status[85].

In Indonesia, although the current legal framework supports equality between men and women, it is very difficult to break down cultural barriers, although several effective programmes supporting women have been implemented. Family Planning and Family Welfare Training stands out as a movement aimed at families in which justice and prosperity prevail. This family planning programme has met with great success in Indonesia, where it has reduced the fertility rate to 2.6 per cent, aiming to 1.2 per cent in the near future[86]. Women leaders of these movements play a central role in the transmission of values and attitudes to the other women. The figures of these chairwomen are a source of confidence and motivation. The current fertility rate in Indonesia is the third highest behind China (1.8) and Brazil (2.3). This situation can be related to the female literacy and primary school enrolment rates that are also high in Indonesia when compared to those of Pakistan, Egypt, Nigeria, India and Bangladesh.

Graph 21: Gender Empowerment Measure (GEM) at the end of the nineties

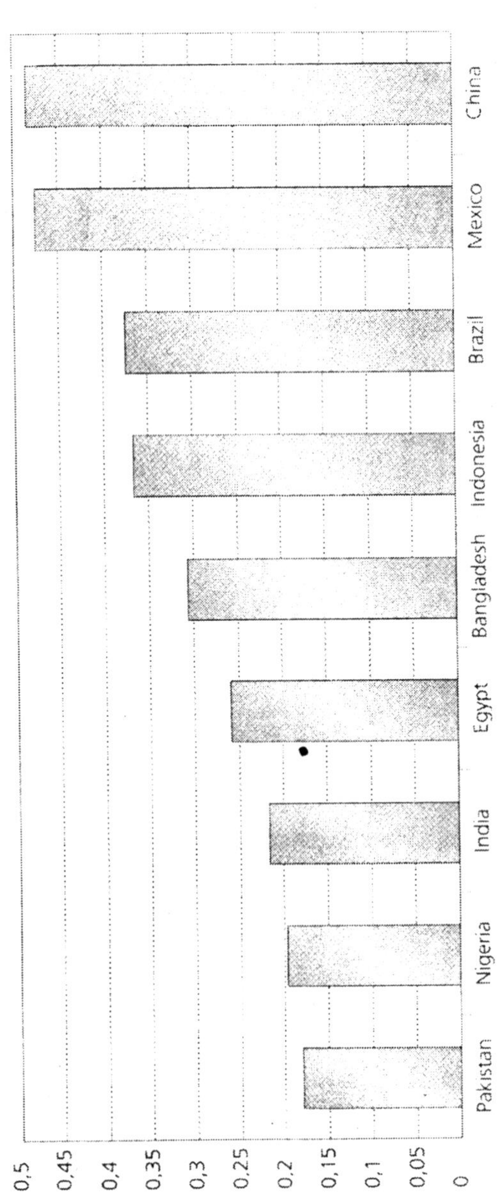

Source: HDR 1998 Gender Empowerment Measure, Internet

Nevertheless, the empowerment of women in Indonesia is very low, due partly to the distribution of work for women in general: 45 per cent work in agriculture and 25.2 per cent in businesses. The remaining working women are distributed among the service sectors (13.1 per cent), industry (15 per cent), construction (0.4 per cent), transport (0.3 per cent), and the electricity sector (0.1 per cent).

Pakistan's gender empowerment measure is 0.179, placing it at the bottom of the list of E-9 countries. Judging by the figures there are very few women who work in Pakistan, at least officially. What's more, they contribute only 21 per cent of the country's revenue. On a national scale, the rate of male administrators is greater than that of women. However, Pakistani women work in the World Bank and in the Asian Development Bank.

Almost 70 per cent of government health institutions have female staff. In the Tehsil hospitals, 22 per cent of workers and 16 per cent of doctors and specialists are women. In district hospitals, 25 per cent of the staff and 14 per cent of doctors are female. There are 7 male doctors for each female doctor in speciality fields. 30 or 35 per cent of women doctors do not practice or else work part-time. Most of them work in the private sector. At the moment (2000), the Social Welfare Minister in Punjab is a woman.

Egypt has a gender empowerment measure of 0.258 for 1995, which puts it in sixth place in the E-9 group. In 1979, a law was passed that allows women to occupy 30 seats in parliament (one for each governorate). The total number of seats occupied by women in parliament is 35 (8.9 per cent of the total).

If the educational level of girls is compared, based on the data available on enrolment rates and empowerment indices, China occupies the top spot among E-9 countries. Additionally, the significantly high rate of continuation secondary school for girls in China is 92.2 per cent[87]. The secondary school dropout rate fell from 3.47 per cent in 1996 to 2.86 per cent in 1998. This direct correlation also occurs in the case of Mexico where a high girl enrolment rate puts it in second place among E-9 countries, in the measurement of gender empowerment.

Pakistan and Nigeria seem to be the countries where women and girls are at the greatest disadvantage in the E-9 countries. In these countries girls have less opportunity to gain access to and remain in school, a lower female literacy rate, lower human development indices, and higher fertility and population growth rates.

GOVERNMENT POLICIES IN FAVOUR OF THE EMPOWERMENT OF WOMEN

Despite the fact that, in some countries, programmes, commissions and committees for the empowerment of women were set up years ago, they have yet to make an impact. Women suffer great disadvantages compared to men in E-9 countries and the gaps between them in terms of equality in educaiton, job opportunities, socialisation, and opportunities for personal growth are still enormous. In this section, some government initiatives in favour of the empowerment of women will be presented, including references to legal frameworks, where applicable.

In Indonesia, policies have been developed based on the principle of equality between men and women. This is stipulated in Article 27 of the 1945 Constitution. Equality is reflected in the inclusion of a special chapter on the role of women in national construction, in the Broad Guidelines of the State Policy 1978. The institutionalisation of the Secretariat for Women's Role in 1978, promoted to Ministry level in 1983, a clear political will to support women[88]. This ministry has been responsible for raising the level of education of women and for developing a socio cultural climate aimed at achieving equality.

Article 12 of the constitution of Bangladesh establishes that the State will take measures to assure the participation of women in all spheres of public life. In 1997, the government launched the National Policy for Women to establish equality betwee men and women, and provide women with education; it aims to prevent discrimination, to put an end to illiteracy, to establish a primary school in every village in Bangladesh, to ensure equal rights for women and girls and to implement special programmes to increase the participation of women in all spheres of educaiton. Strategies have been designed for women's empowerment[89].

The constitution of Pakistan protects women's rights and asures their participation in different spheres of life, as well as eliminating gender inequalities and discrimination. Specific articles prohibit exploitation, abuse, trafficking of humans and prostitution as well as guaranteeing decent working conditions for all human beings. The family is protected and, the participation of women in national life is recomended, as is the representation of women in national government[90].

As for education, the 1994-2000 Social Action Programme stipulates that 60 per cent of schools are for girls, and only female teachers will be employed there.

In Brazil, in the field of leadership training, the CELIM (Centre for Women's Leadership) is coodinated by the Chairman of the National Women's Rights Council.This centre aims to prepare women to exercise political power and participate in decision-making in society as a whole. With support of the IDB, study facilities are offered so that women from all over the country can attend the courses.

In China, the constitution states that women are entitled to the same political, economic, cultural, social and family rights as men. The Proection of Women's Rights and Benefits Act is also in force.

In India, Article 45 of the constitution provides free and compulsory education for boys and girls up to 14 years of age. Article 15 emphasises women and children. The heart of the constitution is formed by two articles related to the fundamental rights of citizens that prohibit any type of discrimination towards women. There have been a series of commissions and committees that attempt to enforce the law. The Commission for Universal Education promotes education for women, claiming that it is impossible to have an educated people if there are no educated women. It states that if education has to be limited to either men or women, it should be offered to women, since in this way it will be passed on to the following generations. Since the late sixties, education policy as aimed to achieve equal opportunities in the education of women, not only for reasons of social justice but also from the conviction that it will accelerate social transformation. The education of women acts as a social catalyst. Consequently, the National Education Policy intervenes in favour of women's empowerment.

Amendments 73 and 74 of the constitution give women power in local government in both rural and urban areas, reserving seats specifically for them. A third of the seats in local government, rural Panchayats and urban environments are now reserved for women.

In Egypt, several women's support programmes have been undertaken, supported by extensive institutional infrastructures. The Pioneer Project trains rural women for work in the Rural Women's Advancement Programme, in order to raise educational, social , and economic standards. Other training projects cover basic skills acquisition, income generation and food production. Furthermore, the Women's Documentation and Information Centre, the Rural Women's Activities Policy and Co-ordination Unit, the General Mother and Childcare Department, the National Women's Committee (created in 1978 and reorganised in 1993, under the auspices of the National Maternity and Childhood Council), all support the cause of women's rights and study their problems. Nevertheless, these institutions seems to have limited impact[91].

The democratic opening-up of Mexico has favoured women's presence in public life and opened new channels for participation at different levels of government as well as in civil society. In Mexico diverse civil groups support the empowerment of women. The work of the National Women's Commission greatly contributes to the inclusion of a vision of gender equality in development policies. In 1998, this commission became the National Women's Council, which, in making the promotion of women a matter of State policy, will transcend the limits of the current administration. The laws of this country include the participation of women in public and political life, with the same rights as men.

In the task of empowering women so that they drive their own development and participate in the progress of society, governments have the obligation to set an example, promoting new rules of coexistence making the connection clear between the problems of women and the problems of society as a whole and by carrying out programmes and actions that promote equality.

CONCLUSIONS

In order to fulfil the objective of universalising basic education, stated in Jomtien in 1990 the nine high-population countries when meeting in New Delhi, India, December 1993, assigned women a central role in educational activities. On the one hand they were responding to their educational debt to girls and women. On the other hand, they were conferring responsibility on women, whether as mothers, teachers, opinion-formers and community leaders, to supervise and administer programmes that guarantee the achievement of basic education.

Progress is evident in all countries except Nigeria. There have been substantial increases in the proportion of girls and boys getting basic education. Literacy rates have constantly risen. In some countries, such as Mexico, there has been a considerable effort to adapt education to the characteristics and needs of groups who cannot regularly attend conventional schools.

This document shows not only the similarities, but also many significant differences between these countries. It also highlights the fact that measures to enhance development adopted by these countries during the 20th century have not always been successful. In rural areas, many practices and beliefs still ignore the rights of women and girls, principally the right to education. However, it is also true that commitment to this educational work continues and that more advances and achievements are likely to be made.

Based on the analysis in this document, the following conclusions are reached:

- Religious, cultural and social ideologies directly affect women's empowerment. The perception of women determines the opening up of opportunities for them. In the most traditional societies, barriers of a religious and cultural nature prevent women from achieving progress outside of the family environment. In such cases, their entry into labour, government, social or academic spheres becomes highly improbable.

- The countries with the greatest inequality in the distribution of wealth, the lowest participation of citizens in decisions that affect national life, and low human and technical development indices, are those where women find it most difficult to progress in any field.
- Mothers continue to occupy a central place in the initial education of their sons and daughters, as transmitters of basic social skills and values and as those responsible for emotional development. However, several countries are re-examining the role of women in the family in order to allow greater participation in the effort for progress.
- The educational level of parents, principally of mothers, determines their sons' and daughters' educational achievement. The higher the level of education of the mother, the greater the chances that their daughters will have access to and remain in basic education.
- In urban areas, the family faces challenges from poverty and lack of access to basic social services.
- In order for woman to achieve optimum development as educators in schools, priority must be given to the following areas:

— Implement in-service teacher training with promotion systems that allow wage rises, without teachers having to leave the community where they teach and live.

— Provide more opportunities to women to gain access to management and administrative positions.

— Provide more and better training so that they can practice their teaching vocation with more professionalism, which will lead to better educational quality.

- In E-9 countries, it has been shown that the higher the level of educational development of girls and women, the higher the indices of female empowerment. The effort that these countries have made to "institutionalise" the progress of women through legal and constitutional reforms, is highlighted by the creation of organisations and institutions that support and guarantee the empowerment of women and girls. Furthermore, when women achieve access to public positions and participate actively in promoting demoractic values, they contribute to the progress of societies.

- The community is the place where the aspirations of the family and the school coincide. Faced with problems of dropout and repetition, it is necessary to reinforce the bonds between the values of the family and the values of school.The challenges of the adoption of democratic values for the peace of nations are challenges for each family and community. The need for schooling to produce educated students is the same need as of the community to have citizens who can address problems of society. Women are essential in bringing these fundamental institutions closer together to achieve a relevant and life-long education for all.
- Each E-9 country, has tested social mobilisation formulas in order to concentrate resources and actions in education for marginalised populations.
- In almost all E-9 countries, women in the most marginalised communities, in rural areas and in cities, have started to organise themselves to supervise and administer the application of government programmes concerning education, health and nutrition.
- The E-9 countries should not relent in their efforts to provide education for all, and to continue to place girls and women at the centre of their national development programmes, because education is our greatest challenge and our greatest hope.

NOTES

CHAPTER I

1. For example, different family models; couples; nuclear families, extended nuclear (4 times), one-parent, extended one-parent, several relatives, co-residents.
2. See the case of Nigeria in the E-9 country studies. In all cases, the concrete references to the countries are taken from the national documents cited in the Bibliography.
3. Gender is understood to mean the group of features assigned to men and women in a society, that are acquired in the socialisation process. These are the responsibilities, rules of behaviour, values, likes, fears, activities and expectations, that culture assigns to men and women in a differentiated manner. In other words, what it means to be a man or woman in a determined culture. From it are derived the different needs and requirements of men and women for their development. Gender is distinguished from the term "sex", as it refers to sociocultural differences and not biological ones. As it is a social construction, it is subject to historical and cultural alterations which derive from changes in social organisation. As a category of analysis, it is fundamentally based on social relationships between men and women". (Gomariz, Enrique. Planning with a Gender Viewpoint. Collection of Methodologies No. 1, National Centre for the Development of Women and the Family. San Jose Costa Rica 1994.)
4. Women in Bangladesh: Their Role as Educators
5. Women in Bangladesh: Their Role as Educators
6. Women in E-9 Countries and their Role as Educators, India

7. Normative and Objective-Empirical Conditions in Selected Development Sectors, Indonesia

8. The Role of Women as Educators in China

9. As Mulheres como educadoras no Brasil

10. Education and the Status of Women in Egyptian Society

11. Egyptian Women as Educators within the Family and the Society

12. Women in Bangladesh: Their Role as Educators

13. Women in Bangladesh: Their Role as Educators

14. As Mulheres como educadoras no Brasil

15. As Mulheres como educadoras no Brasil

16. The data on the gross preschool schooling ratio for Pakistan, India, and China correspond to 1997; those of Bangladesh, Brazil and Mexico are from 1998; the data for Indonesia is not dated. Nigeria and Egypt had general rates of 22.21 per cent (1999) and 10 per cent undated, respectively. (Graph 1)

17. SEP. Profile education in Mexico, 1999

18. In the last decades, some programmes for the care of children of preschool age have been established: Early Child Care Development and Education (ECCDE), carried out with UNICEF; Family Support Basic Education Programme (FSBEP), which includes preschool education initiative of the Nigerian President.

19. Details regarding the general index are: Egypt 1997, Bangladesh, China, Brazil and Mexico, 1998

20. The Role of Women as Educators in China

21. Education and the Status of Women in Egyptian Society

22. Egyptian Women as Educators within the Family and the Society

23. Women in Bangladesh: Their Role as Educators

24. Women in Bangladesh: Their Role as Educators

25. Women in Bangladesh: Their Role as Educators

26. The dates of the indicators have been already stated in previous diagrams, except for the retention to 5th primary school grade. The details of this indicator of Nigeria are from 1996; Pakistan, India, Indonesia and Mexico, 1997; Bangladesh 1998. The general rate of Brazil (65.0 per cent) is from 1994 and the one from Egypt (91.74) belongs to the period between 1991 and 1996 (Graph 3)

27. As mulheres como educators no Brasil

28. As Mulheres como educators no Brasil

29. La Mujer como Educadora, Mexico

30. Women and their Role as Educators in Nigeria

31. The Role of Women as Educators in China

32. The Role of Women as Educators in China

33. SEP. Profile of education in Mexico, 1999

34. As Mulheres como educators no Brasil

35. Women in E-9 Countries and their Role as Educators, India

36. Women in Bangladesh: Their Role as Educators

37. UNESCO. "The E-9 countries: recent demographic trends, literacy rates and UPE: a comment on results, estimates, and projections".

38. For the dates of women's literacy rates see note 27. The details of the male literacy rate for Bangladesh, Nigeria, Brazil India are from 1995; from Indonesia, 1996; Mexico 1997; Pakistan, Egypt, China, 1998. (Graph 6)

39. Theme Paper on Women as Educators, Pakistan

40. Moreover, the decrease of rural population is associated with national processes that have caused the modernisation of structures and markets, encouraging the creation of literate and urbanised areas.

41. The details on rural population were taken from UNICEF and from the E-9 country studies. The details for Brazil are from 1991; Bangladesh, Egypt and India, 1995; Nigeria and Indonesia, 1996;

and Mexico, 1997; others have no dates. Details on drinking water availability date from 1990-96. Details on female life expect in Nigeria, 1993; Brazil, Indonesia, India, Pakistan and China, 1997. All others are undated. Details on female population in Nigeria and Indonesia, 1996; and Mexico, 1997. All others are undated. (Graph 7)

42. Data on infant mortality date from 1996 and were taken from UNICEF. (Graph 8)

43. Women in Bangladesh; Their Role as Educators

44. Women in Bangladesh: Their Role as Educators

45. Gross Domestic Product data are from 1995. China, Egypt and Nigeria data are from National E-9 evaluation papers. (Graph 9)

CHAPTER 2

46. As Mulheres como educadoras no Brasil

47. As Mulheres como educadoras no Brasil

48. As Mulheres como educadoras no Brasil

49. Women in Bangladesh: Their Role as Educators

50. Women in Bangladesh: Their Role as Educators

51. Women in E-9 Countries and their Role as Educators, India

52. Education and the Status of Women in Egyptian Society

53. West African School Certificate (WASC)

54. Women and their Role as Educators in Nigeria

55. Rural population data in Brazil, India and Bangladesh were taken from the UNDP Report 1996. The rest were taken from documents sent by the countries. The data on the rural population of Bangladesh and India are for 1995; that of China and Mexico, for 1997; that of Brazil, for 1991 (Graph 13)

56. The Role of Women as Educators in China

57. The Role of Women as Educators in China

58. Theme Paper on Women as Educators, Pakistan
59. Normative and Objective-Empirical Conditions in Selected Development Sectors, Indonesia
60. See section three of this chapter
61. La Mujer como Educadora, Mexico
62. La Mujer como Educadora, Mexico
63. As Mulheres como educadoras no Brasil
64. Theme Paper on Women as Educators, Pakistan
65. Women in E-9 Countries and their Role as Educators, India
66. The Role of Women as Educators in China

CHAPTER 3

67. As Mulheres como educadoras no Brasil
68. As Mulheres como educadoras no Brasil
69. As Mulheres como educadoras no Brasil
70. SEP. Profile of education in Mexico, 1999
71. Women in Bangladesh: Their Role as Educators
72. 1980-1994 data taken from "The E-9 countries: recent demographic trends, literacy rates and UPE: a comment on results, estimates and projections." 1995-2000 data on Pakistan, Egypt, Nigeria and China were taken from the E-9 country studies. All other data are taken from the mentioned document.
73. Women and their Role as Educators in Nigeria

CHAPTER 4

74. Gender empowerment is understood to mean the control that women are able to gain over their own lives for decision-making regarding their private lives and their involvement in public life and within institutions.
75. The Gender Empowerment Measure indicates whether women are able to actively participate in economic and political life. It focuses on participation, measuring gender inequality in key

areas of economic and political participation and decision making. It thus differs from the Gross Domestic Index, an indicator of gender inequality in basic capabilities.

76. The Human Development Index measures the average achievements in a country in three basic dimensions of human development—longevity, knowledge and a decent standard of living. A composite index, the HDI thus contains three variables: life expectancy, educational achievement (adult literacy and combined primary, secondary and tertiary enrolment) and real GDP per capita.

77. The Role of Women as Educators in China

78. The Role of Women as Educators in China

79. The Role of Women as Educators in China

80. As Mulheres como educadoras no Brasil

81. La Mujer como Educadora, Mexico

82. The gender-related development rate measures achievements in the same dimensions and variables as the HDI does, but takes account of inequality in achievement between women and men. The greater the gender disparity in basic human development, the lower a country's GDI compared with its HDI. The GDI is simply the HDI discounted, or adjusted downwards, for gender inequality.

83. Women and their Role as Educators in Nigeria

84. Women in Bangladesh: Their Role as Educators

85. Women in Bangladesh: Their Role as Educators

86. Normative and Objective-Empirical Conditions in Selected Development Sectors, Indonesia

87. Data included in the National Report for EFA-9

88. Normative and Objective-Empirical Conditions in Selected Development Sectors, Indonesia

89. Women in Bangladesh: Their Role as Educators

90. Theme Paper on Women as Educators, Pakistan

91. Egyptian Women as Educators within the Family and the Society

ANNEX I

EDUCATIONAL INDICATORS AT THE END OF THE NINETIES

Country	Bangladesh	Brazil	China	Egypt	India	Indonesia	Mexico	Nigeria	Pakistan
Territorial Area (km2)	144 000	8 547 400	9 596 960	1 001 450	3 287 590	1 919 440	1 958 200	923 770	796 100
Population density (ha/km2)	873	20	131	67	300	110	51	123	184
Inhabitants (millions)	125,7	168	1254,1	66,9	986,6	211,8	99,7	113,8	146,5
Male-Female (%)	52.5/47.5	49.5/50.5	51.5/48.5	50.7/49.3	51.7/48.3	50/50	49.5/50.5	49.5/50.5	51.7/48.3
Urban/rural (%)	20/80	78/22	30/70	44/56	28/72	38/62	74/26	36/64	32/68
Annual growth rate (%)	1.8	1.5	1	2	1.9	1.6	2.2	3	2.8
Child mortality rate (n/1000)	82	41	31	52	72	46	32	73	91
Income per capita (USD)	360	4790	860	1200	370	1110	3700	280	500
Life expectancy at birth (years)	59	67	71	65	61	63	72	74	63
Male	59	63	69	64	61	61	69	71	62
Female	58	70	73	67	62	65	75	77	64
Gender Empowerment Measure									
Percentage	0,305	0,374	0,483	0,258	0,228	0,365	0,474	n.d.	0,179
Range	80	68	33	88	96	70	37	n.d.	100
Human Development Index (range)	147	62	106	112	139	96	49	142	138

ANNEX II

PRINCIPAL EDUCATION PROGRAMMES IMPLEMENTED SINCE 1990

Bangladesh	• Food for education • Integral development for rural women • School attraction programme	• Infant feeding programme; • Special attention to marginalised women; • Mass adult literacy programme.	• Increase in the number of female teachers throughout the education system; • Increase in the literacy rate from 17 per cent in 1971 to 60 per cent in 2000.
Brazil	• Professional teacher training programmes • PALMAS Project • Education and teaching with gender equality in childhood and adolescence • Landless Movement • School Bag • Textbooks	• Course aimed principally at women; • Literacy for adult women; • Publication of guides and videos for mass distribution; • Social movement including mothers from marginalised areas; • Scholarship programme; • Improvement of content and number of textbooks.	• Mothers in marginalised urban areas look after the children of other working women; • Using the new textbook system, teachers can choose from a list of texts, giving education greater plurality; • General interest of the population in education; • Creation of training opportunities and exchange of experiences for teachers.

(Contd...)

(Annex II. Contd..)

China		• Development of a preschool education network; • Programme to recruit rural girls to work as teachers; • Building of housing for young teachers in rural areas.	• High level of schooling in the whole country, despite a rural population of approximately 70 per cent.
Egypt	• Nile Sat	• Literacy programme using a television channel; • Multimedia and computer programmes for use in schools; • Training through videoconferencing; • One-classroom schools.	• Improvement of the population's response to new technologies and to modernisation in general. • "Excellence for all" campaign to promote the idea that knowledge is a capital; the eradication of illiteracy is not enough.
India	• DPEP (District Primary Education Project)	• Programmes for the education of adults that also promote social and community mobilisation, making them see the importance of literacy	• Social mobilisation with emphasis on education; • Increase in the enrolment rate; • Improvement of general conditions of health and hygiene thanks to access to information.

(Annex II. Contd..)

Indonesia		• Training and education for workers; • Plan of action to improve the quality of women as human resources; • Informal education for dropouts from formal education.	• Enhancing role of mothers in improvement of children's health in marginalised populations.
Mexico	• PROGRESA • SEDENA-SEP-INEA • "Another way to be teachers, mothers, and fathers" • "Education for living together" • Teaching Career	• Education, health and diet; • Adult literacy in partnership with Military Service; • Training and information for parents of preschool age children; • Radio and television programme; • System of horizontal promotion of both male and female teachers.	• The rise in enrolment in secondary education in marginalised areas is due to a large extent to the scholarships of the PROGRESA programme. • Education for life given to conscripts in the SEDENE-SEP-INEA programme is favouring more equal relationships between men and women. • Thanks to the Teaching Career project, female (and male) teachers enter a training and evaluation process of their teaching that allows them to receive better wages and provides students with better classes.

(Contd...)

Nigeria	• FSBEP • FGN	• Basic education programme supporting the family; • Expansion of initial education services.	• Existence of three educational models side by side: traditional, formal, religious
Pakistan	• "Women are educators by nature" • 1994-2000 Social action plan	• Political actions and statements; • Design of general education policies and provision of the means to achieve their objectives.	• More information in the population regarding the role of women as educators; • 60 per cent of new schools should hire only women for teaching posts.

Source : National Reports on the EFA-2000 Assessment.

BIBLIOGRAPHY

BANGLADESH

1) Nurun Nahar Kabir;
   Women in Bangladesh: Their Role as Educators;
   UNESCO, Dhaka, 1999

2) Primary and Mass Education Division, GOB
   The Year 2000 Assessment. Bangladesh Country Report, Dhaka, December 1999

BRASIL

1) Marilia Pinto de Carvalho; Profesora de Education de la Universidad de São Paulo,
   As Mulheres como educadoras no Brasil,
   São Paolo, 1999

2) Instituto Nacional de Estudios e Pesquisas Educacionais,
   Informe Nocional Brasil EFA 2000, Brasilia, 1999

CHINA

1) *The Role of Women as Educators in China,*
   Beijing, 1999

2) *Education for All: The Year 2000 Assessment,*
   Beijing, 1999

EGYPT

1) Rafica S. Hammond;
Egyptian Women as Educators within the Family and the Society; Cairo, 1999

2) *The EFA 2000 Assessment Arab Republic of Egypt*, Cairo, 1999

3) UNESCO Cairo Office
Education and the Status of Women in Egyptian Society, Cairo, 1999

INDIA

1) Champak Chatterji
Women in E-9 Countries and Their Role of Educators, New Delhi, 1999

2) Ministry of Human Resource Development, GOI
Education for All. The Year 2000 Assessment Report, New Delhi, 1999

INDONESIA

1) Ministry of Education and Culture
The Roles of Women as Educators in Indonesia; Jakarta, 1999

2) Nahya. J. Faraz; *Indonesian Women; UNESCO/Mitra Pranata*, Jakarta, 1999

3) Ministry of Education and Culture; 1999
Education for All: The Year 2000 Assessment, Jakarta, 1999

MEXICO

1) Ma. de la Paz López Barajas, Paloma Bonfil Sánchez, MA. De Lourdes Valenzuela y Gomez Gallardo, Cecilia Loria Saviñon
Women as Educators, Mexico City, 1999

2) Ministry of Public Education
General International Relational Department
Jomtien+10 Evaluation of Education For All 2000, Mexico City, 2000

NIGERIA

1) Mrs. Chinyere Ohir-Aniche, M.O.A. Olorunfunmi, 1999
Women and their Role as Educators in Nigeria, Lagos, 1999

2) *Education for All: The Year 2000 Assessment*, Lagos, 1999

PAKISTAN

1) *Theme Paper on Women as Educators;* Islamabad, 1999

2) Ministry of Education, GOP,
The EFA 2000 Assessment Pakistan Report, Islamabad, 1999

UNESCO/Vollmann

The E-9 Countries: Recent Demographic Trends, Literacy Rates and UPE: A Comment on Results, Estimates and Projections, UNESCO, Paris, 1999.

GENERAL

1) Digumarti Bhaskara Rao, Editor
Encyclopaedia of Education for All, 5 Vols.,
APH Pub. Corp., New Delhi, 1996

2) Digumarti Bhaskara Rao, Editor
Education for All: Achieving the Goal, 3 vols.,
APH Pub. Corp., New Delhi, 2000

INDEX